Advertising and Media Management

AF520429

K. Lakshman

S.R. Saritha

Dr. Kiran L Maney

Published by

BONFRING®
Intellectual Integrity

Advertising and Media Management

9 788195 162642 >

ISBN 978-81-951626-4-2

Authors

K. Lakshman

S.R. Saritha

Dr. Kiran L Maney

Bonfring

309, 5th Street Extension, Gandhipuram,

Coimbatore-641 012.

Tamilnadu, India.

E-mail: info@bonfring.org

Website: www.bonfring.org

Preface

We have substantial gratification in presenting the first edition "Advertising and Media Management" written for students of UG Courses. The subject matter is written in simple and easily understandable language with sufficient support from factual information. The objective of writing this book is to provide students with a conceptual framework of Advertising and Media Management, activities of advertising and different advertising strategies.

We consider this book is useful for understanding purposes through students as well as professionals. The book lays down the framework defining the fundamentals of advertising, advertising strategies, Media Management, Media strategies.

This is an attempt to provide the students with through understanding of the advertising and media management. In writing this book we have benefited immensely from the real information of advertising.

This book has mostly concentrated on discussion of the important topics such as history, organization of advertising sector, functions of advertising, online advertising, role of advertising agency, recognized advertising authorities in India and media management.

We are appreciative to various academicians for giving there valuable feedback and support to improve the content in title.

We are highly grateful to Bonfring for taking keen interest at every step in publishing this book.

Any suggestions regarding improvement and errors, if any, will be gratefully acknowledged.

Authors

K. Lakshman

S.R. Saritha

Dr. Kiran L Maney

Acknowledgement

First and foremost, we would like to thank the almighty and his prophet (Peace be upon him). In the process of putting this book together we realized how true this gift of writing is for us. You have given us the power to believe in our passion and pursue our dreams. We could never have one this without the faith we have in your, the Almighty.

We like to thank Our Director Dr. Dinesh Nilkant, JU-CMS, Bangalore, Dr.K.M. Mahesh, Principal SBMJEC.

Our sincere thanks goes to all the Teaching Faculty and Non-teaching Members, Department of Management, Center for management studies, Jain (deemed-to-be) University, Bangalore for their kind support and encouragement.

Words cannot express our deep sense of gratitude for our parents, our family Members, cousins, relatives and Colleagues for their support during my research. We also express gratitude to our friends, for their cooperation during the process of publishing this book.

TABLE OF CONTENTS

CHAPTER I

Introduction to Advertising

- Meaning and Definition of Advertising
- Changing concepts of advertising
- Nature and scope of advertising
- Evaluation of advertising
- Role of advertising in modern society
- Socio and economic impact of advertising
- Advertising in India and Abroad
- Law and ethics in Advertising
- Planning Advertising Campaigns

Meaning of Advertising

- The word advertising is derived from two Latin Words 'Ad' and 'Verto'.
- Ad – towards Verto – I turn.
- Literally it means to turn the people's attention to a specific thing.

Advertising: Advertising is the paid form of non-personal presentation and promotion of ideas, goods, or services by an identified sponsor.

Purpose of Advertising

- To promote ideas about products & services.
- To create interest in products & services.
- To create awareness about products & services.
- To increase sales.

Need of Advertising

Companies use advertising to:

- Inform people about their products and services.
- To make their brand names familiar to the public.
- To give the company a **"personality"** this sets it apart from the others.
- To remind customers about their **brands** at the **right time** and **right place.**
- To tell the public about **improvements** in products.
- To help their sales force to be more effective.

- To reinforce customer confidence in his/her purchase.

Governments and autonomous bodies use advertising to:

- Inform people about their policies.
- Promote birth control.
- Educate the masses on health care.
- Prevent panic during natural disasters.
- Dispel harmful rumors.
- Attract foreign investment.

Public bodies prefer to use professional advertising agencies because agencies have the creative talent to explain complex issues in a way which makes them interesting, easy to understand and meaningful.

Examples: SBI, Bank of India, LIC etc.

Historical Role of Advertising

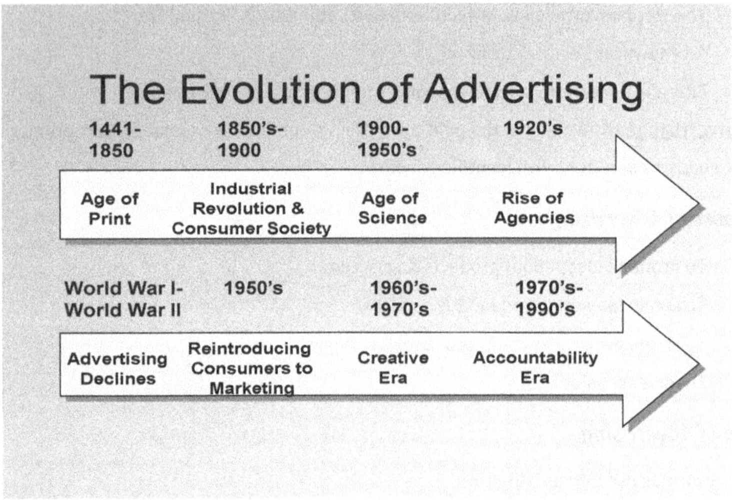

Historical Roles of Advertising

- The Pre-Industrial Age (up to start of 19th century).
- The Industrializing Age (To WW1).
- The Industrial Age (1900's to 1970s).
- The Post Industrial Age (Starting 1980).
- The Global Interactive Age.

a. The Industrializing Age (Mid 1700's Europe / 1800's in U.S. To WW1)
   - Mass production / Need for mass consumption
   - Cost people less to buy products than to make them
   - Manufacturers were concerned with production

b. The Industrial Age (1900's to 1970s)
   - Luxury goods developed
   - Manufacturers changed from a production orientation to a sales orientation

c. The Post Industrial Age (Starting 1980)
   - Age of social responsibility / Quality of life issues
   - Lifestyle advertising

d. The Global Interactive Age (Last 15 years)
   - Growth in world markets

Importance of Advertising

There are several reasons why advertising is an important part of the marketers promotional mixes.

- Firstly, it is very cost effective method to communicate to a large audience.
- Secondly, it helps create brand image and symbolic appeal for the brand which is a very important for companies selling product/services that are difficult to differentiate on functional attributes.
- Another advantage of advertising is its ability to strike a responsive chord with the consumers when differentiation across other elements of the marketing mix is difficult to achieve.
- Popular advertising campaigns attract customer's attentions and can help generate sales. For example Pepsi's – 'Oye bubbly', 'Mere number kab aye ga', Asian Paints – 'Badiaya hai', Alpenleibe -Lage raho, etc.

Some do's and don'ts of Advertising

Some do's

- Advertising should be informative.
- Advertising should be entertaining.
- Advertising should be involving.

Some don'ts

- Advertising should never over claim any benefit in a product or a brand.
- Never try to put down or talk down your consumers in manner that will insult them.

- Try not to compare your brand with a competitor and try not to show your competitor in bad light.

Functions of Advertising

a. **To differentiate the product from their competitors:** An important function of advertising is the identification function, that is, to identify a product and differentiate it from others; this creates an awareness of the product and provides a basis for consumers to choose the advertised product over other products this creates an awareness of the product and provides a basis for consumers to choose the advertised product over other products.

The identification function of advertising includes the ability of advertising to differentiate a product so that it has its own unique identity or personality.

There are four additional ways to differentiate your offering from the competition and increase your differentiation: **leveraging the brand, innovating your service offering,** as well **as designing product** and **packaging** in a way that creates an aesthetic beyond the functional. None of these methods are expensive. All are ways that can increase your perceived value to the customer and increase your market share.

Example: GARNIER FRUTICS (shampoo) the shampoo bottle have the different color from all other shampoo available in the shelf. The bottle of the shampoo is unique from all others.

Example: apple laptops make them different from others as the WHITE color and logo of APPLE on back of the screen.

b. **To communicate product information:** Another function of advertising is to communicate information about the product, its attributes, and its location of sale; this is the information function. Product information communicated to the customers in manner that meets their information needs. Most consumers tend to discount the information in advertising because they understand that the purpose of the advertising is to persuade. Making an advertising message believable is not easy; though often it is sufficient to make the consumer curious enough to try the product. Such curiosity is often referred to as interested disbelief. Advertisers use a variety of devices to increase the believability of their advertising: celebrities or experts who are the spokespersons for the product, user testimonials, product demonstrations, research results, and endorsements.

Example: Ponds age miracle, in that ad the celebrity HADIQA KAYANI is informing the consumers about the benefits of it. That how the old women can look younger by using it continuously. It will make you fair cream plus it reduces freckles plus it can be used as a sun block as well it will make you look young.

c. **To urge product used:** The third function of advertising is to induce consumers to try new products and to suggest reuse of the product as well as new uses; this is the persuasion function. The basic function of advertising is to provide constant reminders and reinforcements to generate the desired behavior the advertiser wants from them. This is a particularly effective function in the long run as reminders and reinforcements register in the consumers' minds, becoming the base on which they shape their future decisions. Sampling in the way to urge the product using.

Example: Fair and lovely as we know that it will make a girl look fair and prettier in 4 weeks.

Example: Neutrogena acne treatment cream will remove your pimple is 24 hours. NEUTROGENA **say no to pimples!!**

d. **To expand the product distribution**: When the consumer comes to know about the particular product from the advertisement he/she wants to try that new product. They go to shops to buy the product; if the new product is not available in a shop then the shopkeeper consults the distributor to make that product available in his shop. It is basically to provide the product all over market. It is necessary to make sure that product should be accessible to everyone. Availability of product effect the distribution.

Example: Wateen telecom and Motorola Partner to Expand Distribution of Videoconferencing Product Line in Pakistan. So as many people are getting to know about this facility they are running towards the franchises to avail it. So for that Wateen should expand their distribution all around the cities.

Accessibility is major factor for successful product

a. **To increase brand preference and loyalty:** Marketing is a moving thing. As your needs are changed your preferences are changed. When the product delivers the promised quality, service and value, it creates satisfied customers who become instrumental in spreading a favorable word-of-mouth. Satisfied customers also develop brand preference; each product features and uses are written on the product.

Example: 99% girls who are not married will not look at the ad of pampers or any milk powder for children but when they will get married their interest will automatically move towards such ad'

b. **Brand loyalty:** Brand loyalty is a long-term customer preference for a particular product or service. Brand loyalty can be produced by factors such as customer satisfaction with the performance or price of a specific product or service, or through identifying with a brand image. It can be encouraged by advertising.

People often make purchasing decisions based on how a brand makes them feel emotionally rather than based on quality or other objective evaluations. If **"Just Do it"** strikes a chord with an athlete, he'll buy Nike; the decision may have little to do with quality.

Example: For instance, when one buys a tube of Colgate toothpaste and finds it ok, one will not have to spend any valuable time on looking for other toothpaste brands.

c. **To reduce overall sales cost:** When a product is selling you have to teach the people about the product.

Like if we would advertise through newspapers, TV, broachers and internet, it would cater huge sum of masses and if you do individually it would be more costly and time consuming.

Example: Coke targets their consumers on a very large scale through mass media whereas Makka cola advertise on smaller scale or go door to door to advertise their product.

d. **Creates new demands:** Advertising have to create new demands they should educate the people about more and more new things coming up in the market. Each year new products, including line extensions and new brands are introduced into groceries and drugstores.

Example: Wateen telecom is offering wireless internet chips, video conferencing and WIMAX services as they are introducing new services in market its creating new demands.

Advantages of Advertising: The various Advantages of Advertising are as under:

- **Increasing sales:** The expenses of advertising may be justified on the ground that it helps to increase sales, which thereby results in increased production.
- **Reduction cost: It** assets to reduce cost of production and distribution which are passed on to consumers in the form of reduced prices.
- **Duplicate advertising: The** basic purpose of advertising is to increase the sales of products which are not in competition, For example large amounts are spent on the publicity of Tooth Pastes which appear to be in competition but which is really produced by the same manufacturers.
- **Prevention of lost sales:** Much advertising is aimed at preventing the erosion of its sales by competitors. So advertising may be regarded as being "defensive".
- **Creating market attitude: Advertising** can create a market attitude for product which would not otherwise be desired. Thus artificial demand can be created by exploiting fears.

- **Impression the public: Advertisement** is considered important branch of business which impresses the public about the superiority of product.
- **Economy in commission:** It introduces the manufacturer in the market as an independent supplier. So public may directly place an order to him which can reduce a wholesaler's commission and utilize it to lower the retail prices.
- **Encouraging competition: It** assists to promote competition among the producers. Thus it facilities to supply goods of improved quality in the market at competitive prices.
- **Increasing business activities: Advertising** helps to increase the business activities in the country. Thus national income and consumption per capita may be increased.
- **Developing goods:** It informs the manufacturers about the changes in taste, fashion and habits of customers. So producer will be in a position to develop his product according to the changed circumstances in the market.
- **Sufficient profit: It** promoters the selling process to the great extent which gives producers sufficient profit.
- **Informing consumers:** Advertising provides the information to consumers about the choice, prices quality and other description of product at their home, which guides them for quick decision.
- **Increasing standard of living: People** are informed about the new scientific inventions, new style and use of products. Improved accommodation, better clothing and food by advertising. Thus it stimulates the desire of public which increases their standard of living.
- **Providing employment: As** it helps to create the new demand of the products, it tends to increase the sales volume of goods. So new industry will be established and old industry will be expanded where thousands of persons may be engaged.

Demerits of Advertising (Objections)

Various objections against it may be listed as follows:

1. Economic Objections

a. Advertising is not productive. It is true that it does not produce any tangible goods. It is said to involve wasteful expenditure.

b. It forces people to desire and buy goods, which, in fact, are not within their means.

c. It increases the cost of goods. Advertising charges are included in the price, which the consumer has to pay.

d. Advertising results in monopoly. The consumer becomes a slave to a particular brand.

2. Social Objections

a. Most of the advertisements contain tall claims and the consumers do not enjoy the benefits advertisement in full. They are short lived only.

b. The press is influenced by the advertisers because they provide major revenue for the existence of newspapers.

3. Ethical Objections

a. Advertising appeals make people to use such articles, which may affect their health. For example alcoholic drinks and cigarettes.

b. People with less purchasing power cannot afford to buy articles even though advertisements create a strong need in them. Thus a section of society remains discontented. Whatever may be said against advertising, it is increasingly used almost in every branch of business to promote sales. It is not merely a means of sales promotion but today it has become a science equivalent to any other social science.

ROLE OF ADVERTISING IN MODERN BUSINESS WORLD: Advertising plays an important role in today's modern business world. The role of advertising are broadly consists of three important functions they are as under:

a. Economic Function

- Advertising communicates the message in persuasive language.
- It create wide markets as the information is delivered to people far and wide.
- It inclines people favorably to the products and affect our attitudes.
- Therefore, advertising performs an economic function by being an art of persuasion.
- Advertising is also an economic process—it helps the product to become known and it facilitates exchange between those who need the product and those who can satisfy the need.
- Provides employment opportunities (in advertising industry).

b. Social Function

- Advertising affects the core cultural values and subsidiary cultural values.
- Advertising is a mirror to the society in which it operates...it reflects the cultural values of that society.
- Advertising can also transfer some cultural values of one society to other.
- Advertising has improved our standard of living.

c. *Psychological Function*

- Advertising is closely linked to consumer behavior, therefore,
- It affects personality of consumer, his concept of self, his attitudes, beliefs, opinions, his life-style etc.
- Advertising appeals to our physiological and psychological motives.

Changing concept of advertising: Advertising management is strictly a system of interacting organizations and institutions that play a role in advertising process. At the core of this system are advertisers. Advertisers and organizations who provide the financial resources to support advertising. Advertisers may be private or public sector organizations that make use of mass media to accomplish marketing and organizational objectives.

Advertising management is heavily focused on the analysis, planning, control and decision making activities of the advertiser. Though there exist number of facilitating institutions that are involved in the advertising process, it is the advertiser provides the overall managerial direction and financial support for the development of advertisement and the purchase of media time and space. The advertiser develops an advertising programme or plan. In case the advertiser offers several products, a separate advertisement program may be developed for each media. The resulting schedule of exposures is referred to as an advertising campaign. The development and management of an advertising campaign associated with an advertiser's brand, product or service is thus a major point of departure for advertising management. "Thus *advertising management is one of the marketing functions that relates to planning, organizing, direction and controlling the advertising programme with the involvement of a number of controlling and facilitating institutions"*

Factors Responsible for Changing Concept of Advertising

a. **Globalization (Integration of world economy)**: Integration of world economy means being business globalised. The business houses and big corporations are going globally in business and trade transactions. The marketing in global context is more complex and contains many critical faces so the advertising is also being challenging.

b. **Government regulations**: government regulations are also being imposed and code of conduct for the advertisements is being a popular habit of nations. It is also changing the advertising practices.
c. **Increasing competition**: Today the cut throat competition, prefect market and homogeneous products and services are also forcing the advertisers to make their presentations creative, innovative and different from others in order to make uniqueness in the communication.
d. **Technological Developments**: The technology, media services and other supporting facilities for advertising are developing day-by-day and these are providing the full room to make the advertisements distinguished and more effective.
e. **Other factors**: Other factors like educational level and life standard of people, literacy rate, changes in preferences and tastes are also responsible for changes in advertisement.

In developing and managing an advertising campaign, the advertiser basically deals with numerous institutions as illustrated below.

A company out sources its advertisement needs to three support or facilitation agencies- the advertising agency, the media and research suppliers. The advertising agency and the research agency assist the advertiser in analyzing the opportunities and threats, creating, testing and selection of ideas. These agencies also guide in buying the right media time and space.

Government and competition are the two most important external control institutions which interact and affect the advertiser's decision making activities in a number of ways. Most advertisers are affected by a wide range of government regulations concerning their products, services and advertising. For example, Cigarette marketers have to give statutory warning "Cigarette smoking is injurious to health" on all cigarette packages and advertisements. Similarly direct or indirect competitors also serve as a major external control. What competitors do and how they react is an important part of advertising management.

The group of customers that an advertiser is attempting to reach through advertising is yet another external institution that both facilities and controls advertising. Groups of customers could be housewives, professionals, voters, patients, kids, government etc. these groups are a controlling force through a wide range of behavioral possibilities such as viewing or not viewing, buying or not buying, etc. since it is the customer, to whom advertising campaigns are directed, for whom media are used and advertising agencies create copy and on whom advertising research is done, the identification and understanding of markets and consumer behavior is thus also a vital part of advertising management.

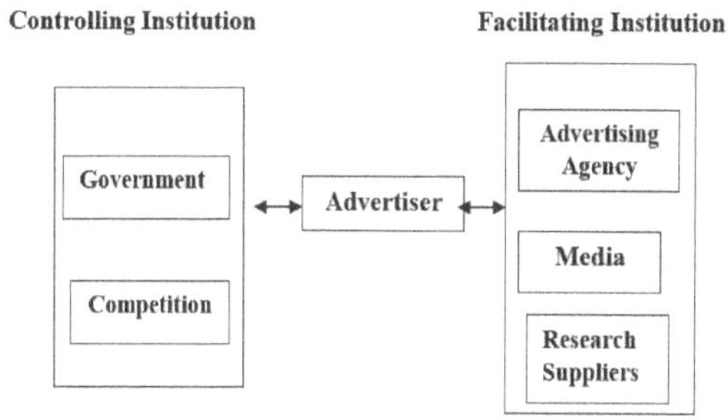

Social and Economic Aspects Advertising in the Marketing Mix Relation to Profits

Economic Aspects

a. **Effect on the value of products or services:** Advertising sets off a chain reaction of economic events. Why do consumers prefer advertised brands compared to unadvertised brands in the same product category? Not necessarily because advertised brands are superior but because advertising can add value to a brand in the consumers mind.

b. **Effect on prices:** It seems logical to think that if advertising adds value to products or services it also adds cost and affects price. And in case companies stop this expensive advertising, products would cost less and would be available at lower prices. This is a major area of continuing debate among economists' advertisers, consumer advocates and policy makers. This view is not totally correct.

c. **Effect on Consumer Demand and Consumer Choice:** It is generally agreed that the effect of advertising and other promotions increase aggregate consumption, but to what extent it affects consumption, there is disaggregate on this issue.

d. **Effects on competition:** Economists have a common criticism about advertisement that it creates a barrier to entry of smaller firms with less resources who cannot match the power of large firms with huge advertising budgets. High costs may inhabit the entry and brands of large firms probably benefit greatly from this barrier. This results in less competition and increases the prices. Smaller firms, already operating in the market find it difficult to compete against industry leaders and are often compelled to leave the business.

For Instance, with the entry of Pepsi and Coca- Cola, domestic soft drink companies had to abandon the business.

Social Aspects of Advertising: The source of controversy over advertising systems from the way it is used by advertisers. In accomplishing the sales or communication objectives of marketers, advertising influences social values, lifestyles and society's tastes. It is criticized for being untruthful or deceptive, offensive or in bad taste and exploits vulnerable groups.

Social Issues in Advertising

a. **Cultural and value Issues:** Advertisements' must cope with culture environment and value systems of the society. Otherwise they will not be acceptable for the society and they will be opposed and create adverse impact on the promotion objectives.

b. **Standard of Living:** Advertisements enhance the standard of living of the society by providing the information about new and innovation products for use. To make life comfortable smart and easy. But at the same time it is criticized on the basis that society is forced by advertisement to purchase something beyond their limits as status symbols and it creates disturbance and extra burden for people.

c. **Knowledge to society:** Advertisements provide knowledge to the society about the products and services produced and distributed about the different business organization. The decision making of an individual becomes sharp in presence of adequate options.

d. **Society Government Chain:** advertisements work as a chain between government and society and the policies and issues concerned with welfare and development are communicated by government by the help of advertisement.

It is generally agreed that advertising exerts a powerful social influence and is criticized for encouraging materialism in society. It is also blamed for manipulating consumers to buy things for which they have no real need, depicting stereotypes and controlling the media.

Planning an Advertising Campaign

- An **advertising campaign** is a series of advertisement messages that share a single idea and theme which make up an integrated marketing communication (IMC). Advertising campaigns appear in different media across a specific time frame.
- The critical part of making an advertising campaign is determining a *champion theme* as it sets the tone for the individual advertisements and other forms of marketing communications that will be used. The campaign theme is the central message that will be communicated in the promotional activities. The campaign themes are usually developed with the intention of being used for a substantial period but many of them are

short lived due to factors such as being ineffective or market conditions and/or competition in the marketplace and marketing mix.

- Certain businesses choose to advertise when their **target audience** is most likely to buy their product or service. Sometimes this can be seasonal - a toy retailer, for example, will focus much of its advertising efforts around the run-up to Christmas. If you're selling to other businesses, it's worth identifying when your customers and potential customers will have the budget to spend.
- However, some businesses choose to focus more attention on their quieter times on the basis that the busier times will naturally see an increase in sales. Advertising during quieter times might mean you won't have to work as hard to stand out from other competitors, as they won't be advertising, but there may be fewer customers to target.
- Gaining a greater market share during these periods could not only help during the busier times - as you will have already developed a bigger customer base - but will improve your cash flow and minimise your reliance on certain trading periods.

The Reasons behind a Campaign

1. Many businesses launch advertising campaigns simply to **boost sales** or **increase brand awareness**.
2. The launch of a **new product** will almost certainly require you to step up your advertising.
3. **New businesses** will want to consider some form of advertising just to let people know they exist. You could consider an introductory offer to give people an incentive to visit or call.

- **Advertising Ethics**: A set of moral principles that guide actions and create a sense of responsible behavior.
- **Advertising Ethics:** Moral principles and values that govern the actions and decisions of an individual or group.
- **Six key issues in Advertising Ethics**
  - Poor taste and offensive advertising.
  - Stereotyping.
  - Body and self-image.
  - Targeting children.
  - Misleading claims and other message strategies.
  - Controversial products.

Advertising in India and Abroad

- According to Zenith Opt media, the global advertising expenditure in 2004 was approximately $371 billion, out of which out-of-home accounted for just 5.3 per cent, which would put it at around $ 19 billion. But if we look at similar figures only for Western Europe -- the most developed outdoor market in the world -- then out-of-home would account for around 10 per cent of the ad spend in those markets.
- In comparison, according to a Pitch – Madison Advertising Outlook 2005, the Indian outdoor industry was worth Rs 800 crore in 2004. It had grown by 10 per cent over 2003 and accounted for around 8 per cent of the total ad spends in the country. So, even though outdoor advertising as a percentage of ad spends and in terms of year-on-growth seems healthy, we must understand that we are talking about a very small base here. But thanks to big outdoor spenders like the telecom, financial services and the entertainment industry, all indicators are still quite encouraging.
- Billboards are a part of American life, in recent years, with about 1,500 digital billboard displays Traditional roadside billboards remain the predominant form of outdoor advertising in the US with 66 percent of total annual revenue. Today, billboard revenue is 73 percent local ads, 18 percent national ads, and 9 percent public service ads.
- Out-of-home advertising (or outdoor advertising) is made up of more than 100 different formats, totaling $6.99 billion in annual revenues in 2008 in the USA.

Top Spender in Advertisement

- **Microsoft** – more than 20 percent of their annual revenue or $11.5 billion
- **Coca-Cola** – more than $2.5 billion
- **Yahoo** – more than 20 percent of their annual revenue or $1.3 billion
- **eBay** – 14 percent to 15 percent of its revenue – which was $871 million, much of that to advertise on Google
- **Google** – In the millions rather than billions of dollars – with $188 million
- **Starbucks** – $95 million

COMPANIES IN ADVERTISING

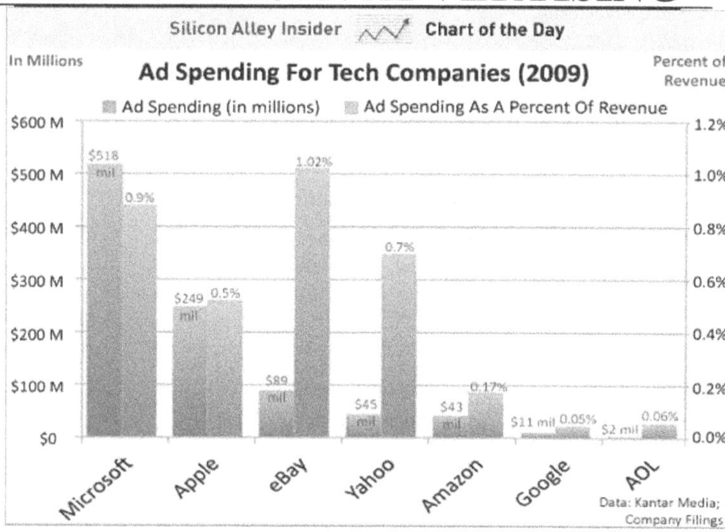

www.businessinsider.com

Module 1
Lakshman K

58

Innovation in Advertising

- Innovation can be defined as the application of new ideas to the products, processes, or other aspects of the activities of a firm that lead to increased "value." This "value" is defined in a broad way to include higher value added for the firm and also benefits to consumers or other firms.
- The recent excellent innovative campaign are: Vodafone Zozo and net connect, DOCOMO, Uninor, MicroMAX unplugged, aircel rain protection campaign and Ree flek etc.

Excellent Innovation in Outdoor

- Absolut Vodka scores big again in the originality department! This billboard appeared on a Manhattan street with the entire contents of a studio apartment attached to it. Add in the cross-promotional aspect by having all the contents from IKEA (check out their mobile advertising in our ad labs) and you have a sure-fire winner.
- To create a completely stunning design, keeping in mind the different taglines of the clients. The communication initiative was to make a design in order to convey the exact thought of the client and increase awareness about brand presence.

Model Questions

a. Define advertising.
b. What is advertising?
c. Explain the various functions of advertising
d. Explain the various do's and don'ts of advertising.
e. Explain the various advantages and disadvantages of advertising.
f. Explain the role of advertising in modern business.
g. Explain the evaluation concept of advertising
h. Explain the need of advertising
i. Explain the importance of advertising.
j. Explain the various changing concept in advertising.
k. Explain the various social and economic impacts of advertising
l. What is advertising campaign? Explain the reasons behind campaign.
m. Explain the various types of advertisement.
n. What is advertising agency?
o. Bring out the comparison of Advertising in India and Abroad.
p. Explain the role of innovation in advertising.
q. What is Advertising Etics? What are the key issues in advertising Ethics?

CHAPTER II

Types of Advertising

- Types of Advertising, Product, Services, Institutional, Public services, Financial and Industrial.
- Online Advertising.
- Types on Online advertising.
- Impact of Online advertising in today's Business.

Types/Classifications of Advertising

Classifications of Advertising

By Target Audience	By Geographic Area	By Medium	By Purpose
• Consumer • Business	• Local (retail) • Regional • National • International	• Print • Broadcast (electronic) – Radio – TV • Out-of-Home • Direct-Mail	• Product • Non product • Commercial • Noncommercial • Action • Awareness

1. Product-Related Advertising

a) **Informative advertising**-This advertising figure heavily in the Introduction stage of a product, where the primary objective is to build demand.

Example: MOTOROLA Ads for pagers & Mobiles, explaining how to use them (providing information).

b) **Persuasive advertising-** Persuasive Advertising figures heavily in the Growth Stage of Product Life Cycle, where the company's objective is to build selective demand for a particular brand. Like- AKAI TV ads compared the brand with 6 competitor brands.

c) **Reminder advertising-** This advertising is highly important in the mature stage of the product to keep the consumer thinking about the product.

Example - Fevicol campaigns act as a reminder form of advertising, bonding Fevicol with consumers as the strongest Adhesive.

2. **Trade Advertising**- It can classify into two categories:-

- Retail advertising

- Wholesale advertising

a. **Retail advertising-** can define as covering all advertising by store that sell good direct to the consuming public. Example- in & out promotional techniques of retail outlets.

b. **Wholesale advertising-** Wholesalers are, generally, not advertising minded, either for themselves or for their suppliers. They would benefit from adopting some of the image making techniques used by retailers.

3. **Area based advertising**:- There are three types of this advertising. They are as follows-
   a. **National advertising-** This type of advertising is to encourages the consumer to buy their product wherever they sold. Advertising that is done in one nation only. Dabur Ads or Nirma Ads.
   b. **Global Advertising**: Advertising that is carried on for a company or a product globally. Like- I'm loving it was a global ad released by McDonalds.
   c. **Local advertising**-Advertising that is carried out in a particular region or market. Like-BRU and AMRUTANJAN selected campaign directed towards consumers in South India.

Other types of Advertising

4. **Manipulative advertising**:- "limits free and informed action."It is sort of like convincing customers to purchase something, but it is based on incorrect or inconclusive information.
5. **Surrogate advertising**:- Surrogate advertising is prominently seen in cases where advertising a particular product is banned by law. Advertisement for products like cigarettes or alcohol which are injurious to heath are prohibited by law in several countries and hence these companies have to come up with several other products that might have the same brand name and indirectly remind people of the cigarettes or beer bottles of the same brand.

Like- "aap, main or Bagpiper". This Bagpiper club soda advertisement, featuring cine celebrities, is similar to the earlier one for Bagpiper whisky.

6. **Unethical advertising**: - Unethical advertising is when you promise something you cannot deliver. For Example- In the fitness industry, you advertise that you guarantee a weight loss of 50 pounds per month with your program. You cannot possible deliver that to every person who comes into your gym.
7. **Covert advertising**:- Covert advertising is when a product or brand is embedded in entertainment and media. Covert advertising is a unique kind of advertising in which a

product or a particular brand is incorporated in some entertainment and media channels like movies, television shows or even sports.

For example, in a film, the main character can use an item or other of a definite brand, as in the movie Minority Report, where Tom Cruise's character John Anderson owns a phone with the Nokia logo clearly written in the top corner, or his watch engraved with the Bulgari logo.

8. **Brand advertising**: This advertising helps in the long-term build up of a brand. It is advertising with a strong emphasis on the company brand (logo and/or company name) also known as integrated marketing communications (IMC).

Example: HLL's ad's for LUX, LIRIL, REXONA.

9. **Classified Advertising**: Is a product or services advertising that appears in specific section of newspaper under the heading classifying the product or service being offered. This advertising gives information dissemination about a sale. Example:MID-DAY NEWSPAPER or TOI classified section.
10. **Promotional Advertising:** This advertising informs an announcement about a sale. ADIDAS offering 50% DISCOUNT on sneakers.
11. **Advocacy Advertising**: This advertising is used to publicize a particular cause. All the social ads fall into this category. Drink, MORE MILK (TV ad by FCB ULKA for NDDB) & AIDS AWARENESS ADS by Govt.
12. **Negative advertising**:- emphasizes on negative attributes of the competitor's product instead of focusing on positive attributes of own products.

Example.- Horlicks Vs. complain, Pepsi Vs Thumps up

13. **Public Service Advertisement:** The same advertisement techniques use to promote commercial goods and services can be used to inform, educate and motivate the public about non-commercial issues such as HIV/AIDS, Political ideology and Energy conservation.
14. **Financial advertising**:- Ads taking only about finance related things. Example- all insurance ads.
15. **Gorilla advertising: -** Guerrilla Advertising is an unconventional way of performing promotional activities. Usually very funny or subtle, it's a great way to promote a business with a low budget and generate buzz. But you'll need lots of creativity.
16. **Non-Product Advertisement**: This kind of advertisement is advertised from political parties' trade fraternal and social group for the purposes of safeguard ideologies, social betterment and institution.

17. **Out-Door Advertisement**: Bill-board and message painted on the side of buildings are common forms of out-door advertising, which is often used when quick, simple, ideas are being promoted.
18. **Celebrities Advertisement**: Although the audience is getting smarter and smarter and the modern day consumer getting immune to the exaggerated claims made in a majority of advertisements, there exist a section of advertisers that still bank upon celebrities and their popularity for advertising their products.
19. **Infomercials Advertisement**: There are two types of infomercials, described as long form and short form. Long form infomercials have a time length of 30 minutes. Short form infomercials are 30 seconds to 2 minutes long. Infomercials are also known as direct response television (DRTV) commercials or direct response marketing.

Example: Teleshopping Products Advertisement, Telebrands Advertisement.

20. **Industrial Advertising:** Advertising directed at commercial business customers. The advertised products are raw materials, components, or equipment needed in the production or distribution of other goods and services.
21. **Professional advertising**: Advertising directed toward professionals such as doctors, dentists, and pharmacists, etc., who are in a position to promote products to their patients or customers.

Online Advertising

One major benefit of online advertising is the immediate publishing of information that is not limited by geographic or time constraints. Online advertisers can customize advertisements, making consumer targeting more efficient and precise. For example, AdWords, Yahoo! Search Marketing and Google AdSense enable ads to be shown on relevant web pages or alongside related search results. On the other hand, consumers have greater control over the content they see, affecting the timing, placement, and visibility of online advertisements. Within the scope of Internet marketing, online advertising includes display advertising, affiliate marketing, search engine marketing (SEM), and mobile advertising.

Types of Online Advertisement

Display Advertising

Display advertising is the use of web banners or banner ads placed on a third-party website or blog to drive traffic to a corporate website and increase product awareness. These banners consist of static oranimated images, as well as interactive media including audio and video. Display advertising uses demographic and geographic targeting - capturing users' cookie and browser history to determine demographics, location, and interests - to target appropriate ads to those browsers.

In addition to contextual targeting, online advertising is targeted based on a user's online behavior. This practice is known as behavioral targeting. For example, if a user is known to have recently visited a number of automotive websites based on clickstream analysis enabledby cookies stored on the user's computer, that user can then be served auto-related ads when they visit other, non-automotive sites.

Social Network Advertising

Social network advertising is a form of online advertising found on social networking sites such as Face book. Advertising on social media networks can take the form of direct display ads purchased on social networks, self-serve advertising through internal ad networks, and ad serving on social network applications through special social network application advertising networks.

Search Engine Marketing (SEM)

Search engine marketing is a form of marketing that seeks to promote websites by increasing their visibility in search engine result pages (SERPs). SEM tactics include paid placement, contextual advertising, and paid inclusion, or free search engine optimization techniques to drive placement of their ads. Advertisers pay each time users click on their listing and are redirected to their website, rather than for the ad itself. This system allows brands to refine searches and gain information about their market.

Mobile Advertising

Cell phone advertising is the ability for organizations and individuals to advertise their product or service over mobile devices. Mobile advertising is generally carried out via text messages or applications. The obvious benefit of mobile advertising for brands is that mobile devices such as smart phones are usually close to the owner throughout the day. This presents a cost-effective way for brands to deliver targeted advertisements across mobile platforms on a daily basis. Technologies such as location-based advertising also give marketers the ability to deliver ads in close proximity to the physical location of a consumer. Although advertisements appear on a small mobile interface, mobile advertisers have the ability to deliver personalized, and thus effective, messaging.

Google AdWords (Pay-per-click Advertising)

Pay per click advertising is an excellent alternative for companies who have the financial resources and can make an investment in order to bring targeted traffic to their websites. Like SEO traffic, AdWords is considered targeted because people are actually typing in keyword phrases that are relevant to your products and services before clicking on your advertisement. This can bring a flood of traffic to your online business very quickly, and this is an excellent choice as long as you are able to turn a profit.

Banner Advertising

This form of online advertising is even older than the search engines themselves, and the concept is pretty simple. You simply put some sort of banner (usually with a catchy image and headline) on a relevant website. Users who choose to click the banners will end up on your website and hopefully will make a purchase. The problem is that these days, web users have developed "banner blindness" so only a small percentage will actually click on your ad.

PPC Ads

PPC ads, AKA pay-per-click ads, are advertisements in which the cost of advertising is determined by the number of clicks an ad receives. Ad Words and Bing Ads both use a pay-per-click model.

Bing Ads

Bing ads are similar to Google ads in that they work on a pay-per-click basis. Advertisers can manage their ads through the Bing Ads service, formerly known as Microsoft adCenter. You can get started with creating Bing Ads here once you have a Bing Ads Account.

Face book Ads

Marketplace ads appear in the side columns of the Face book website with a headline, copy, and an image.

Promoted Posts are Face book ads that let advertisers pay a flat rate to promote a single post on their Face book business page. The promoted post reaches more fans and friends of fans than a regular post.

Sponsored Stories show a user's interaction with an advertisers page or product to the user's friends and larger network. Sponsored Stories are also one form of Facebook ads that can appear in a user's newsfeed.

Twitter Ads

Twitter ads refer to the paid boosts that brands on Twitter can use to extend the reach of their tweets, promote a chosen hash tag, or gain more followers.

Promoted Tweets lets advertisers' tweets reach more people's home feeds, and offer a healthy batch of targeting options. Twitter ads also include Promoted Accounts, letting advertisers show up more often in Twitter's who to Follow recommendation feature. Promoted Trends gets your custom hashtag in the Trends bar, earning additional attention and notice from the Twitterverse.

In-Game Ads

In-Game ads are advertisements that exist within computer or video games. One of the most common examples of in-game advertising is billboards appearing in sport games. In-game ads also might appear as brand-name products like guns, cars, or clothing that exist as gaming status symbols.

Email Ads

Email ads are advertisements sent to users via web mail. Email ads can be used to notify subscribers of certain promotions, discounts, or new features, among other uses.

Most email advertisements feature a large image with minimal text; users will not waste large amounts of time reading email ads, so it's important to make your message as clear and concise as possible. Email ads also rely on a compelling subject line to ensure that a user will open the email.

Gmail Ads

Gmail ads in Google's online email service are contextual ads that are generated by an automated process that scans a user's emails to discover interests and topics that are relevant to the user. If a user is writing and receiving many emails about air conditioners, that user may see ads about air conditions appear within the Gmail client.

While privacy advocates are wary of such practices, Gmail advertising is fully automated and Google asserts that no humans read user emails, only robots.

Video Ads

Video ads are growing in popularity as better internet speed performance and online advancements make it fast and easy to watch videos on the web. The most successful video ads avoid blatant advertising, opting instead for educational, how-to video content that naturally appeals to users, with some (if any) product suggestions discreetly integrated.

YouTube Ads

YouTube ads are ads that appear on Google's video-sharing site. Since Google obtained ownership of YouTube, advertising on YouTube has become nearly as easy and customizable as advertising on AdWords.

YouTube ads provide a number of targeting options and several different ad formats. YouTube advertisements can appear as banner ads, in-video overlay ads, in-stream video ads (which are video ads that appear before or during another YouTube video), as well as several other setups.

Content Marketing

Content is the King for any online advertising and marketing campaign, and it has a influential role on the success of any website or online marketing campaigns. A good, unique and informative content is accepted by all types of users and also has a better chance of getting promoted virally over the internet. So if you have the right content and proper content marketing strategies, then your success will have no limits.

Benefits of Online Advertising

The number of internet users is on a rapid rise worldwide and the internet is being used by people of all age and types. Internet has become one of the major medium for communication, entertainment and is indeed in the process of replacing traditional entertainment, promo products, and informative medias. Some businesses are finding that handing out a promo product such as pens, business cards, and mugs are too costly and yield little results. Likewise, traditional marketing forms such as television, radio, newspaper, magazines, etc., are becoming a thing of the past.

Internet has also undoubtedly become a major and effective medium for advertising and it can clearly be predicted that the online advertising and marketing is very soon going to replace the advertising through traditional medias such as television, radio, newspaper and magazines. Most of the companies and organizations are relying on digital advertising and marketing techniques to improve their overall sales and revenue.

The advantages of online advertising are many when compared with the traditional advertising and marketing techniques. The online advertising and marketing scenario is drastically entering a wider area and in the coming years one cannot even think of a business promotion without the help of internet advertising. Here I have picked around 10 advantages of online advertising (not in that order) when compared with the traditional offline advertising.

1) Wider Coverage

The online advertising gives your ads a much wider global coverage and this helps in making your online advertisements reach more audiences, which may ultimately help you in getting better results through your online advertising campaign. With internet advertising, you can also specify the range of your advertisement coverage which helps you to enjoy a better advertisement campaign.

2) Targeted Audiences

When compared with offline advertising, online advertising always helps you to reach the targeted audience and this helps in making your campaign more profitable and getting more relevant leads.

3) Affordable

Another main advantage of online advertising or marketing is the much affordable price when compared with the traditional advertising costs. With a much lesser cost you can advertise on the net for a wider range of audience and geographical locations.

4) Easy to Track and Measure Conversion

Measurability and easiness to track the conversion makes online advertising miles ahead on the traditional advertising methods. A lot of effective analytics tools are available to measure online advertising campaigns which help in more improvisation of the ads.

5) Speed

Online advertising is faster than any of the offline advertising activities and you can start sending out your online ads to a wider audience, the moment you start your advertising campaign. So if you have a large targeted audience online at the time of triggering your online advertisements, then your ad will be served to majority of the audience in no time.

6) Informative

In online advertising, the advertiser is able to convey more details about the advertisement to the audience and that too at relatively low cost. Most of the online advertising campaigns are composed of a click-able link to a specific landing page, where users get more information about the product mentioned in the ad.

7) Flexible Payment

Payment flexibility is another added advantage of online advertising and marketing. In offline advertising you need to pay the full amount to the advertising agency irrespective of the results. But in online advertising there is the flexibility of paying for only qualified leads, clicks or impressions.

8) Better ROI

Since online advertising is mainly focused on performance based payment, you ROI is sure to be far better when compared with offline advertising. You can also easily track and analyze the performance of your online advertisements and adjust them so as to improve your ROI.

9) Easy Audience Engagement

Most of the online advertisement platform makes is easy for the audience to engage with your ads or products. As an advertiser we would be able to get more feedback from the audience and thereby improve the quality of our ads going forward.

10) Better Branding

Any form of advertising helps in improving the branding and online advertising stands a notch high in improving the branding of your company, service or product. If your digital advertising campaign is well planned, you have the chances of getting your brand name spread virally over a larger audience.

Disadvantages of Online Advertising

The disadvantages of online advertising are less, but they exist:

Intrusive ads. The nature of a lot of online advertising ads and campaigns is intrusive, that's why browsers' pop-up blockers can frequently prevent ads from being presented. Almost all browsers now block pop-ups. There are also extensions available for the Chrome, Opera and Firefox browsers, which will block ads on websites. More and more consumers use these methods to avoid seeing so much the advertising.

Copyright problem. Your advertising materials are automatically available for everyone in the world. They can copy it, regardless of the legal limitations. Trademarks, pictures and logos can be copied and used for commercial purposes. In traditional advertising, such as TV, radio and newspaper advertising, where pictures must be replicated, copying the content is much more difficult.

Technical Obstacles

The nature of a lot of display advertising is intrusive, so pop-up blockers can often prevent ads from being served as they were intended by the advertisers. Most browsers now block pop-ups. There are also extensions available for the Firefox browser, such as Adblock Plus, that will block advertising on Web pages. Technologically savvy consumers are increasingly using these methods to limit the advertising that they see.

Connection Speed

Bandwidth can also be an issue, although this is a shrinking problem. However, campaigns should be planned around demographics in determining the richness (and investment) of interaction. For example, heart disease medication is likely to appeal to an older community with less money and slower connection speeds.

Advertising Fatigue

Consumers are suffering from advertising fatigue, so while new technologies can provide great results, as soon as the market moves mainstream, it can get saturated. Consumers are increasingly ignoring advertisements.

Overloading of Ads in a Webpage

- All advertisers would want to compete to grab web users' attention resulting in a cluttered webpage. Usually, web users would ignore the ads due to the overload of information on a webpage.

Pop-up Ads

- These ads are known to annoy web users because it interferes the users activity on a webpage. Many web users ignore these ads or use pop-up ad blockers to get rid of them.

Slows Down Webpages

- Animated or embedded games on ads grab web users' attention but it will load slower compared to static ads.

CHAPTER III

Advertising Planning and Decision Making

- Advertising Planning & Decision Making, Planning Frame work
- Marketing strategy and situational Analysis
- Marketing Plan and advertising, Communication Process
- DAGMAR Approach
- The Advertising Plan, Facilitating Agency, Personnel selling
- Sales Information, Publicity, Identifying Prospects
- Ad Appeals, Other Functions of Advertising, Stimulating and Expanding Demand

Learning Objectives

- Learn about major components of the advertising plan.
- Understand the importance of setting objectives.
- Discuss the success factors of introductory advertising and the relationship between advertising and sales.
- Discuss various budgeting methods used in advertising.

Impact of Advertising

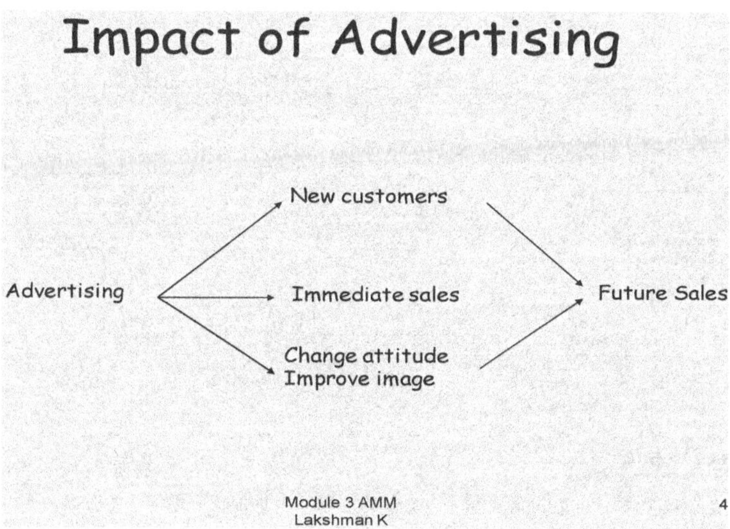

Advertising Plan

An Advertising Plan Matches the Right Audience to the Right Message and Presents It in the Right Medium to Reach That Audience & Has Three Elements.

- Targeting the Audience: Whom are you trying to reach?
- Message Strategy: What do you say to them?
- Media Strategy: When & where will you reach them?

Meaning of Advertising Plan

- Detailed outline of a firm's or a product's advertising campaign which shows what are the advertising objectives, how they will be achieved, and what commitment of resources is required.

Developing an Advertising Plan

- Advertising objectives and target market selection.
- Creative plan: Message strategy and tactics.
- Media plan: media strategy and tactics.
- Evaluation (research).
- IMC approach: identify roles of various forms of IMC and repeat the process.

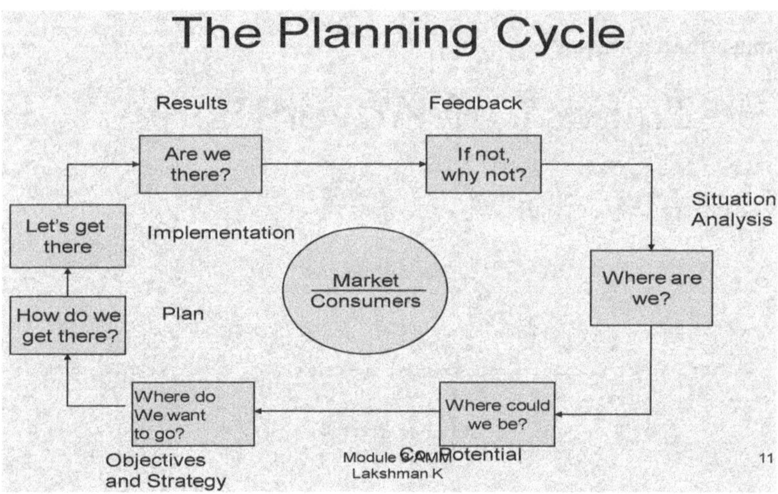

Whose job is it?

- Advertising Planning is done by marketing department.
- Normally the brand manager.

- In some cases it could be the advertising manager, the marketing manager, the product manager and similar designations.

Role of the Brand Manager in Advertising Planning

- CEO of the brand.
- Accountable for the sales, profits, contribution and fortunes of the brand.
- Needs to interact with all functionaries, internally and externally and do whatever it takes to ensure the progress of his brand.

Reasons for Advertising Plan

- Represents an outgrowth of the marketing plan.
- Organizes the marketing plan's situation analysis into a SWOT analysis.
- Sets advertising objectives.
- Determines advertising strategy.
- Sets budget.

Need of Advertising Plan

1. Effective advertising lowers your cost of doing business.
2. Minimal, limited duration, or random advertising equals wasted money.
3. Advertising is not creative or funny if it does not bring in clients.
4. Advertising has a cumulative effect, and is a long-term investment. Sales response builds over time if advertising is consistent.
5. With consumer goods and services, marketing and advertising affects your market share more than price does.
6. Effective advertising comes from solid planning and high quality production.
7. Synergy is a real thing in advertising. It comes from the cumulative effect of all of your marketing materials working together.
8. There are limits to what advertising can accomplish, even with an unlimited budget. Advertising cannot make up for poor quality, service, or timing.
9. Every company should go through the advertising planning process.

Advertising Plan Components

Step 1: Introduction

- Executive summary
- Overview

Step 2: Situation Analysis: The most important factors that define the current situation and then explain the importance of each factor

- Historical context
- Industry analysis (supply)
- Market analysis (demand)
- Competitor Analysis

Step 3: Objectives

- To create or maintain brand awareness.
- To change consumer beliefs or attitudes.
- To influence purchase intent.
- To stimulate trial use.
- To convert one-time users into repeat purchasers.
- To encourage brand switching.
- **Sales vs. Communication Objectives**: *Focusing on communications objectives allows advertisers to consider a broad range of strategies. Building brand loyalty can take years.*
- combining sales and communication objectives can be an excellent way of evaluating an advertising campaign.
- **Step 4: Budgeting Methods:** The company uses different types of budgeting methods based on there requirement. Some of the important Budgeting methods are as under:

a. **Percentage of sales:** Does not relate spending to objectives.
b. **Share of market/voice:** Likely to maintain "status quo" market share.
c. **Response models:** Depends on sales = advertising relationship.
d. **Objective and Task:** Preferred and strategic.

Step 5: Formulating Strategy: the company will formulate the strategy according to the requirement and they go for execution next step in advertising Planning.

Step 6: Execution: Copy strategy (manner by which the creative objectives will be accomplished)

- Media plan
- Integrated brand promotion

e. **Step 7: Evaluation**: How will you track sales? How will you link sales to advertising? Who, in your company or with the client, will do that?

- Direct response and Internet advertising is easy to track.
- Branding focused campaigns may not be easy to link to sales. Talk to a research company if you want to do that.

- Here's a tip: Capital One spent over 100 million annually, mostly on TV ads, to build brand recognition during the early 2000s. That's the kind of money it takes to buy a nationwide brand. What's in your wallet?

Media Planning is another important phase of advertising campaign after creative strategy i.e. preparation of right message. Until and unless, the message is communicated through the right medium to the target consumers, the message is of no use. So deciding about the correct place (where) and the time (when) is very important to carry out the advertising objectives, hence media Planning.

Media Planning is the process of designing a course of action that shows how advertising time and space will be utilized to contribute to the achievement of marketing and advertising objectives. Media Planners are responsible for preparing the media plan from information about the market and the prospective consumers. This information are collected through market research. Media decisions are primarily based on two variables

a. The creative strategy established for the campaign, and
b. The characteristics of the target Market.

The creative strategy developed for the advertising campaign may require that certain media be employed or more likely, the advertiser may have a strong preference for certain type of media to be used in communicating the massages. Obviously, these factors influence the media decisions and should be considered when media are being selected.

The second important factor is target market. Facts about the target market is gathered through market research and generalized into consumer profile. The consumer profile alone with the basic copy strategy and copy requirements as modified by any need for seasonal or geographical emphasis and taking into account the size of the advertising budget is then analysed by the media planners.

The analysis is, then followed by matching the audience characteristics of various media with the consumer profile and by evaluating the adoptability of the physical format of the media to the copy requirements. Thus, through the exercise of judgment concerning the dimensions of coverage, reach, frequency, continuity and ad size, the media plan emerges.

In media planning, the help of advertising agency may be sought or this work may be delegated to it. The advertise will, in most cases, review the media plan as developed by the agency and approve it finally before it is implemented. Advertising agency has specialist media planners and they recommend for specific media.

Three decisions are made during the media selection Process

i. The general type of media is chosen, newspaper, magazine, radio or TV
ii. Class within the chosen type are picked –spot or network, television, general or particular type of magazine and
iii. Specific media vehicle. Within the chosen class of the preferred type is selected.

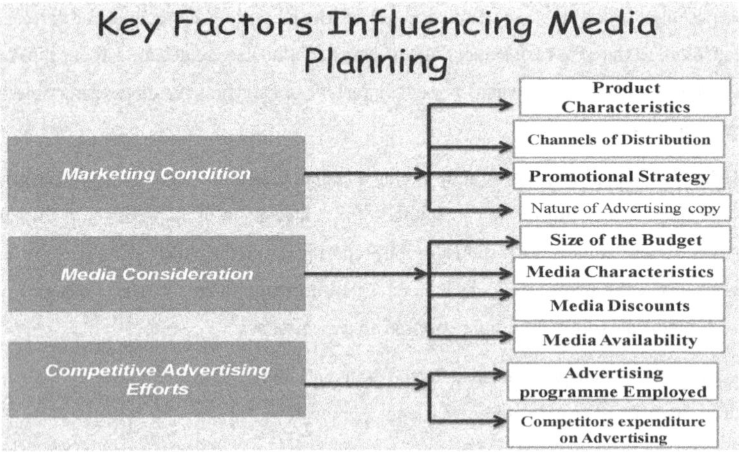

There are so many factors that influence the media planning. These factors may be grouped into three major

a. Marketing conditions facing the advertiser.
b. The level of competitive advertising efforts, and
c. Specific Media considerations.

1. **Marketing Conditions**: Marketing conditions, to a great extent, influenence the marketing plans of the advertiser that in turn, influence the advertising plans. Media plans are likewise affected by what the firm hopes to achieve in the market place through the use of advertising. In addition, three are four other facts to consider when assessing marketing conditions- Product characteristics, distribution channels, promotional strategy and the nature of advertising copy.

   a. **Product Characteristics**- Product characteristics also decide the media to be used by the advertiser, certain specific characteristics may disqualify its advertiser to use a particular medium.

   b. **Channels of distribution** – Most Products can be promoted through any type of media but factors other than product characteristics must be considered. Geographical distribution of goods or different channels or distributions are other points worth consideration. If the product is distributed locally or regionally, the media that may cover those markets may be more useful.

c. **Promotional Strategy**: There are various parts of promotional mix- advertising personal selling, sales promotional or pubic relation, the advertiser or the planners must coordinate all these parts so that interdependence may exist among them. if an advertiser wishes to promote the sales of the product to consumers, any sales promotion device should be advertised aggressively to make it successful.

d. **Nature of advertising copy**- The advertising message itself play an important part in making choice for the advertising media. The message or the campaign themes may be designed for universal use, i.e. they may be adapted to almost every advertising medium or the themes may be developed only to suit the specific media.

2. **Media consideration**: Advertising media possess certain dimensions that affect the media decision. In deciding the media objectives, various factors have their impact on media decision. These factors are a) size of the budget, b) special requirements to be found in media concepts of reach, frequency, continuity and dominance, c) Media discount, structure d) cost efficiency of different media and e) availability of media to advertiser.

    a. **Size of the Budget**: The size of the advertising budget, i.e. amount allocated for the advertising activity puts and upper limit on the advertising efforts of the advertisier.the smaller the size of advertising budget, the more difficult task, it will be to make media selection decision because small budget advertisers cannot afford any wastage in their advertising programme and they must wrong every paisa of selling power form their advertising.

    b. **Media characteristics**: in developing media objectives, the four major inherent characteristics of the media should be considered- reach, frequency, continuity and dominance. The first two – reach and frequency are undoubtedly the most critical factors in media decisions while other two are less important.

'Reach' is related to coverage i.e. the number of people who are exposed to the message at least once during a stated period (may be a week or a month).

'Frequency' is the numbers of members of the audience are exposed to the advertising message. When the advertiser wants a high rate of reach many media vehicles are to be engaged simultaneously.

'Continuity': Continuity of advertising means many things. For instance, it related various advertisements in an advertising programme too one another. This is important because isolated ads generally make little impact.

'Dominance' Dominance has been defined as 'superior to all other'. In advertising dominance means size and length of the message unit. Full page advertisements are considered to be more dominant than half pages and usually serve as a determinant of true reach as opposed to potential reach.

c. **Media discounts:** having considered the type and class of media, the advertiser may select an advertising media because of the discounts offered by the media owners. Few national advertiser use only one medium or one class of media regularly and they get a handsome discounts compared to offers given by other media owners. The savings in this way is better utilized to enhance the readership through better quality ads i.e. colors may be used or larger space can be utilized.

d. **Media cost Efficiency:** very often the advertisers want to carry the message to the largest number of audience and thus attain an economy in cost of advertising per audience. They compare the total audience with the total cost and take this ratio as the base and choose the most efficient medium. In such cases, advertisers ignore quality approach and play only a 'number game'. This basis is satisfactory if all other factors are balanced out.

e. **Media Availability:** The availability of or time space may also determine the media choice. This factor is more relevant in television. Often, the advertiser could not use the media because suitable time slat is not available. Sometimes, an advertiser who has not planned to use television in his programme may plan to use it if suitable time is made available. The same principle is applicable to other media. Thus, there are certain media considerations that play a decisive role in media decisions.

3. **Competitive Advertising Efforts**: One important goal of every marketer is to design a marketing programme that may retain or improve his market share. Advertising is one of the forces used to achieve this goal, but it is more apparent gauge of competitive activity than the work of a competitor's sales force or distributive organization. It is more difficult to find concrete information about these two areas of competitive activity. Thus the success of an advertiser can be ganged on the basis of two factors

a. Advertising programme employed.

b. Competitor's expenditures on advertising.

Planning Framework: In media planning several factors are considered. Different types of information are gathered, analysed, evaluated, weighed and thought over and then a comprehensive media plan is prepared. The following key factors need to be covered in a comprehensive media plan are as under:

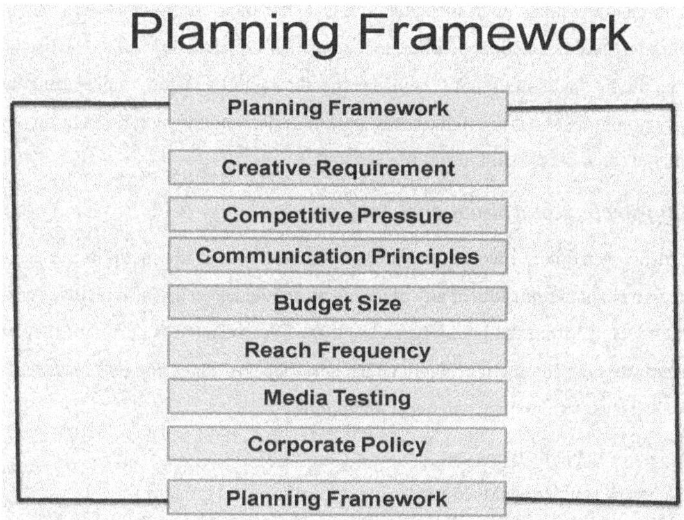

- **Creative requirement**: It represent the message objective, target audience, basic creative Promise and style of Presentation. Taking these creative requirements into mind, the advertiser prepares the media Plan that aims at effective communication and persuasion of the message to the target audience through advertisement.
- **Competitive Pressures**: Every advertiser desire to capture a share of the market. In this attempt, he always try to influence the readers and viewers to switch over to his brand and thus to snatch a sizable part of the market.
- **Communication Principles**: the main principles of communication are clarity, brevity, understandability and Knowledge.
- **Budget Size.** Budget size deals with spending advertising amount where the business is and takes into account such factors as geographical, seasonal and prospects differences.
- **Reach and Frequency**: Reach means coverage of the media or the number of customers to be benefited or exposed by the message. Frequency is the number of times the target audiences are exposed to the advertising message.

- **Media Testing**: In order to have an effective media plan a continuous review is necessary. Through regular review of the plan, they may come to know whether media objectives achieved.
- **Corporate Policy**. They next consideration in designing media plan is a corporate policy. The media planner must recognize the fact that their recommendations should be in agreement or not against boarder policy consideration laid down by advertisement firm.

In brief, the media planners must consider the above stated factors in preparing the media plan. Every point must be given a due consideration otherwise the money spent on buying the media will not fetch the maximum return expected.

Marketing Strategy and Situational Analysis

Advertising scheduling involves the problem of selection of the media types i.e., whether magazine or newspaper or radio or any other media should be used, it also involves what media should be selected within the media types i.e., if the advertising, it is pertinent that he should also concentrate himself on the problem which newspaper or magazine will serve his purpose. So, we shall discuss two main problems of scheduling

i. Selection of Media types and
ii. Selection of individual medium within a specific media type.

Procedure in selecting Media Type

The media planner has to know the capacity of the major media types to deliver reach, frequency, and impact. The major advertising media along with their costs, advantages, and limitations are to be well understood. Every media plan requires that specific media types be selected - Doordarshan, Direct mail, satellite TV, newspapers, magazines, etc. Media planners must consider several variables before choosing among major types:

Target -audience Media Habits

This is the most important factor. Housewives watch more of television, whereas, working women go for magazines. Again television programmes have different viewers. For instance, "world this week" is viewed by teenagers and young adults. Therefore, it would be advisable to advertise during "World this week" such products which are of interest to teenagers and young adults. Radio and television are the most effective media for reaching teenagers.

Products

Products that require demonstration can suit for television. For example, the demonstration of the use of a vacuum cleaner by Eureka Forbes. Financial advertising such as new issue of shares is good in newspapers. Women's dresses are best shown in color magazines, and Polaroid cameras a best demonstrated on television. Media types have different potentials for demonstration, visualization, explanation, believability, and color.

Again there are media restrictions on certain products. For instance, alcoholic drinks and cigarettes cannot be advertised in press as well as on DD and AIR, hence these two options are totally ruled out.

Message

The type of message dictates the type of media. For example, an ad that features technical information is best suited for specific magazines. Again, an ad from retailer announcing major sale on discount requires more of local newspapers.

Cost Factor

Television is very expensive, where as, radio is very economical. However, cost is not the only factor, even if it is calculated on the basis of cost per- person reached. The impact of the media is to be taken into account.

Difficulties in Selecting Media Type

The procedure of selection of advertising media type is not so easy as it is taken. Various considerations are there which make the selection difficult. The main difficulties faced by advertiser while considering the selection of media type are

a. **Difficulty in Audience Measurement**: The success of advertising is on the point how many audiences were exposed to the advertisement in a specified time. This depends on the media because media sell circulation or the opportunity to develop circulation.
b. **Difficulty of cost comparison**: There is a cost per thousand concepts in every medium type for the advertiser but the basic unit varies, sometimes being cost per thousand homes or thousand viewers or thousand passersby or per page per thousand copies sold.
c. **Reliance of manufacturer**: The next difficulty in selection the media type is to determine how much reliance a manufacturer should place on a particular type of medium. In other words how much of his promotion efforts should a food manufacturer place in magazine and how much on radio or TV. How much, if any in outdoor or point of purchase? He is also to decide which type should be dominant and which one supplementary?

Media costs- The cost of space and time, are the largest single expense item in most advertising budget. The following matters should get attention are

i. **Availability and suitability**- Availability of a particular media in a particular region need attention. A media not available at a particular place cannot be selected for advertising.

ii. **Selectivity**: some big sales ideas demand visual presentation, some others demand oral presentation. The radio cannot accommodate stores requiring stores requiring a physical form in such cases print media or television will be most suited.

iii. **Competition:** The advertiser cannot ignore the media used by the competitors. He can select the same media as used by competitors on its being effective. On the other hand, the advertiser can make a unique choice of some other media not used by his competitors, counting on distinctiveness and domination to justify the choice.

Marketing Plan and Advertising

Definition: A **marketing plan** is a business document written for the purpose of describing the current market position of a business and its marketing strategy for the period covered by the marketing plan. Marketing plans usually have a life of from one to five years.

Purpose of a Marketing Plan

The purpose of creating a marketing plan is to clearly show what steps will be undertaken to achieve the business' marketing objectives.

While some small business owners include their marketing plan as part of their overall business plan, if a business owner follows the recommended SBA format, parts of the marketing plan will be included in the various areas of the business plan. As an alternative, the marketing plan may be attached in its entirety as an appendix to a business plan.

What's in a Marketing Plan?

A typical small business marketing plan might include a description of its competitors, the demand for the product or service, and the strengths and weaknesses from a market standpoint of both the business and its competitors.

Other elements usually contained in a marketing plan include:

- Description of the product or service, including special features.
- Marketing budget, including the advertising and promotional plan.
- Description of the business location, including advantages and disadvantages for marketing.

- Pricing strategy.
- Market segmentation (specializing in specific niche markets or, if mass marketing, how marketing strategy might differ between different segments, such as age groups).

Importance of Marketing Planning

If you are just starting out, this is one of the most important activities you will do. Just like a business plan is vital, a thoroughly-researched marketing plan will ensure you give your new business the best possible chance at survival.

If you are well down the track with campaigns in place, don't become complacent; a marketing plan is only effective when it is up to date and relevant. It is quite common for established companies to permanently file the plan, or to allow plans to become so out of date they no longer reflect current activities or new media options.

Costly errors can occur because time is not spent on the critical tasks of planning, ongoing research, testing, measuring and evaluating against the objectives identified in the company's marketing plan. Ideally the plan should be viewed as a living document; it should be updated, changed, referred to and constantly reviewed to ensure the activities are reaching the desired outcome.

A marketing plan does not have to be complex or overly lengthy, but it should clearly:

- Define the objectives and priorities of your business.
- Identify your products and services, prices and the profit margins of each.
- Determine your placement, market position, industry and competition.
- Generate a unique selling proposition.
- Identify the ideal customer profile and how to locate such customers.
- Plan optimal promotional strategies and tactics.
- Identify strengths, weaknesses, opportunities and threats.
- Determine the optimal marketing budget.
- Estimate the marketing return on investment (ROI).
- Evaluate the effectiveness of your marketing campaigns.
- Include an action list with timeframes and allocation of resources.

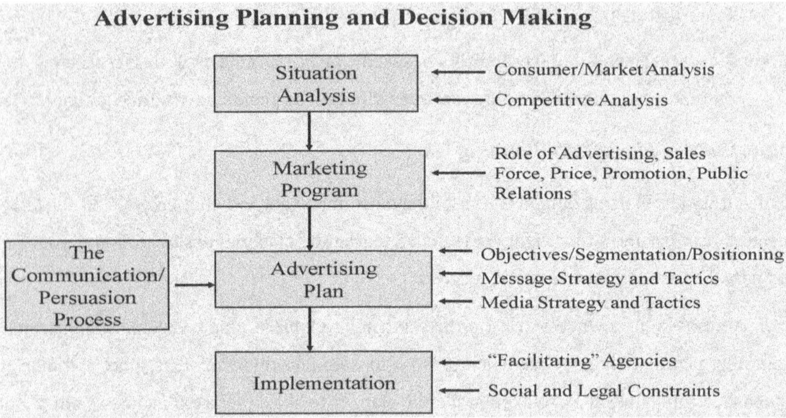

The Planning process of Advertisements Campaigns includes the following Activities

1. **Situation Appraisal-** before planning any activity, one requires relevant information regarding the situation. For planning an Ad campaign, we require information about the target market or consumer, the company or product and the competition. The three important research areas are:
   - Consumer research and market research.
   - Product and company research.
   - Competitive research.
2. **Situation Analysis-** (analyzing strengths, weakness, opportunities and threats) from all the information collected, campaigns planners find out the strengths of the product. These strengths could be in any area. The strength often leads to new opportunities to be explored. Weaknesses make the product vulnerable to threats from others.
3. **Structural or Strategic Planning-** Advertising is an art and a science. While the art comes from writing, designing and producing exciting advertisements, the science comes from scientific methods of research and strategic planning. Strategic planning is the process of making intelligent decisions. It starts with finding out what to do, deciding how to accomplish the objectives. It also decides whom to address (the target audience), how to distinguish the product, how much to spend (budgeting), and how long to run the campaign.
4. **Creative Planning-** it includes developing a theme, the creative strategy and finally deciding the creative tactics. The theme needs to be a strong concept to be able to hold all there different and diverse ads together. A powerful theme brings about 'synergy' to

the campaign. A theme must always relate to and reflect the campaign objectives. Another step of creative planning is finding the creative strategy. The creative strategy outlines the impressions the campaign wants to create. Some common creative strategies are:

- Generic Strategy- this is used by market leaders who ignore the presence of competitors.
- Pre-emptive claim strategy- here the brand is the first to pick up a particular feature. In the minds of the people, it becomes associated with that brand.
- Unique selling proposition (USP) strategy- here the campaign talks about some features, which is unique to that advertised brand and is not available in others.
- Brand image strategy: when there are no strong differentiating features among the competitors, then branding try and create images.
- Product Positioning- some times products or brands are positioned different from competing brands.

5. **Media Planning-** the ultimate goal of advertising is to reach the target audience with the advertising message. Thus, the major decisions in media planning, which needs to be taken, are:
    - Which media to be used?
    - Where to advertise (geographic region)?
    - When to advertise (timing and scheduling)?
    - How intense the exposure should be (frequency)?

Media planning is a 'behind the scene' part of advertising. It plays an integral role in merging the science of marketing with the art of advertising. A media planner has to find out about the availability of various media, the media rates, their reaches and also analyze their effectiveness.

The Dagmar Approach

- Define
- Advertising
- GOAL for
- Measuring
- Advertising
- Result
- DAGMAR Approach is the task of measuring ad effectiveness as well as the objectives or goals of advertising.

- In 1961, Russel H. Colley wrote a book under the sponsorship of the association of National Advertisers called Defining advertising goals for measured advertising result. The book has become know as the DAGMAR approach.
- Colley distinguished 52 advertising goals that might be used with respect to a single advertisement.

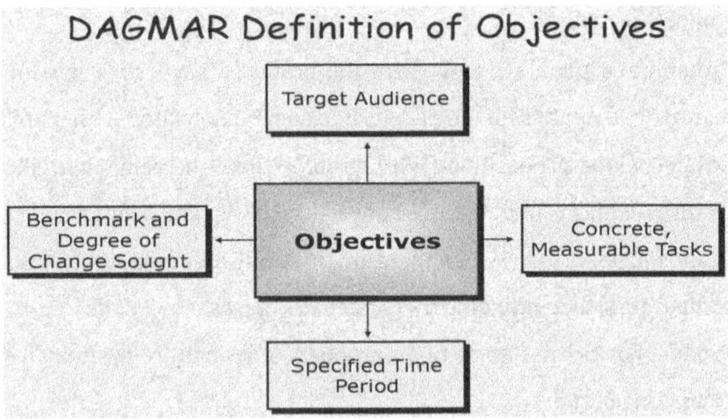

Goals of DAGMAR Approach

The goals may pertain to sales, image, attitude and awareness. Some of the goals are:

- Persuade a prospect to visit a show room & ask for a demonstration.
- Build up the moral of the company's sales force.
- Facilitate sales by correcting false impression, misinformation & other obstacles.
- Provide information regarding benefits & superior features of brand.

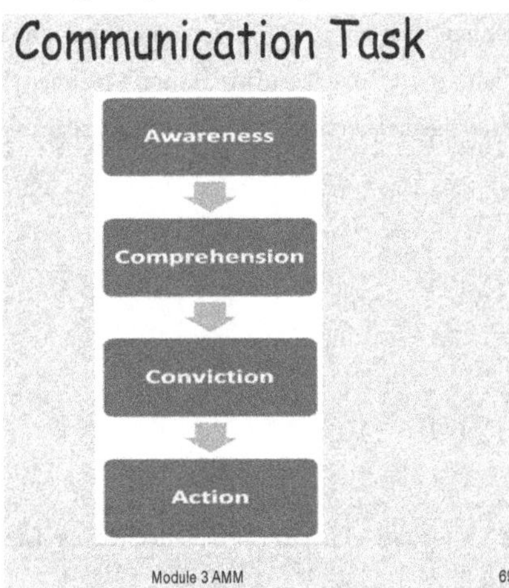

- **Awareness: Awareness** of the existence of a product or organization is necessary before the purchase behavior can be expected.
- Once the **awareness** has been created in the target audience, it should not be neglected. If there is neglect, the audience may become distracted by competing messages and the level of awareness of focus product or organization will decline.
- **Awareness** needs to be created, developed, refined or sustained, according to the characteristics of the market and the particular situation facing an organization at any one point of time.
- **Comprehension:** Awareness on its own may not be sufficient to stimulate a purchase. Knowledge about the product or the organization is necessary. This can be achieved by providing specific information about key brand attributes.
- In attempting to persuade people to try a different brand of water, it may be necessary to compare the product with other mineral water products and provide an additional usage benefit, such as environmental claims.
- The ad of Ganga mineral water, featuring Govinda, which banked on the purity aspect. They related the purity of the water with that of river Ganga.
- **Conviction:** The next step is to establish a sense of conviction. By creating interest and preference, buyers are moved to a position where they are convinced that a particular product in the class should be tried at the next opportunity.
- To do this, audience's beliefs about the product have to be moulded and this is often done through messages that demonstrate the product's superiority over a rival or by talking about the rewards as a result of using the product.
- *Many ads like Thumbs Up featured the reward of social acceptance as 'grown up'. It almost hinted that those who preferred other drinks were kids.*
- **Action:** Communication must finally encourage buyers to engage in purchase activity. Advertising can be directive and guide the buyers into certain behavioral outcomes,
- *Use of toll free numbers, direct mail activities and reply cards and coupons.*
- *Tupperware, Aqua Guard, are famous in Indian cities as a result of its personal selling efforts.*
- For high involvement decisions, the most effective tool in the communication mix at this stage in the hierarchy is personal selling. Through the use of interpersonal skills, buyers are more likely to want to buy a product than if personal prompting is absent.

Characteristics of Objectives

The second importance concept of DAGMAR approach is that the advertising goal should be specific. It should be consists of:

- Measurement procedure: To indicate exactly what appeal or image is to be communicated and to specify the measurement procedure.

CHAPTER IV

Advertising Agency

- Advertising Agency, Origin development of the agency, organisation, structure, functions and departments.
- Client and agency relationship.
- Advertising Budget.
- Evaluating advertising – Research.
- Some typical and Agency Problems.

Advertising Agencies: Advertising agencies specialize in the field of developing preparing and executing commercial advertisements.

- They provide counsel, relative to the designing of ads and allied operations of its clients.
- It is that organization which provides specialized knowledge, skills and experience needed to produce effective advertisement campaign.

American Marketing Association: describes ad-agency as: Independent business organization.

- Composed of creative and business people.
- Who develop prepares and place advertising on media.
- Who work for sellers seeking to find customers for their goods and services.

Functions of Advertising Agency

a. **Advertising development and creative function:** This is the most important function of advertising to develop the ad according to the requirements of the company. In this function all the creative works are done.

b. **Media selection:** media selection is also a function it is also very important to determine the reach, frequency and effectiveness of advertising media. Ad agency does this function for their clients in the limits of budgets and on the basis of target audience.

c. **Research and development:** Being in the direct contact with the customers, advertisement agency has to do the proper research work to know about the habits of consumer and their attitude concerned with jobs. The performance of past and prevailing ads is also studied critically.

d. **Communication of the Advertisement:** Advertisements are communicated by ad agencies for which their services are indeed taken.

e. **Relationship function:** advertisement agencies work like a mediator in between client and media as well as target audience. These develop their relations very sound with all the concerned parties, so making relation with concerned parities is also a function.

f. **Recording and Data Maintaining:** Maintaining the records of the performance of the advertisements is also a function of ad agencies on the basis of which all functions can be performed very efficiently.

Advantages of an Advertising Agency: The various advantages of Advertising agency are as follows:

1. **Developing Campaigns**: An advertising agency will work with the business to develop a campaign. This can involve everything from coming up with a promotional theme, determining the proper media to use, creating the ads, and even negotiating the prices for purchasing the advertising with the various media. This can be extremely beneficial to the business owner who has little or no advertising knowledge or has only used one type of media.

2. **Creative Expertise**: While business owners may be experts in their particular field, they may possess little or no knowledge of what makes an effective, attention-grabbing advertisement. Advertising agencies are staffed with people whose sole job is to come up with innovative ideas that can be completely original, or based on themes that have worked in the past. This can also help the business owner who is not inclined to think creatively.

3. **Market Research:** Business owners may not be strong in the area of market research. The advertising agency can perform much of the legwork in this area by helping to identify the business's target market as well as their key demographics. Thus, the advertising agency may be better suited to determine what type of advertising would be most effective, as well as to whom the ads should be aimed.

4. **Save Time and Money:** With many small business owners being pressed for time, it is often not feasible for them to carve the necessary time out of their busy day to create a full-blown advertising campaign, even if they possess the expertise to do so. Also, if they don't know what they are doing, they can end up spending a lot of money on advertising that proves to be ineffective. While hiring an agency can result in an additional expense, this can be offset by the return on the investment resulting from a well-planned and executed campaign.

5. **Branding:** An advertising agency can be instrumental in helping a business develop a recognized brand. Agency artists can develop logos and other design features that can become of a part of the business's advertising. It can also help with tailoring the brand so the business can meet the unique challenges of marketing the brand on the Internet.

Disadvantages of Advertising Agencies

- **Additional Expense:** Hiring an advertising agency is an expense that some businesses cannot afford, especially during tough economic times. When you hire an ad agency, you're tapping into the expertise of copywriters, designers and creative directors, all of whom need to be compensated from the commission you pay. For many small businesses, an advertising agency is not an affordable option.
- **Unfamiliararity with Your Product**: The ad agency may know toothpaste or iPods or microwaves, but it may know little or nothing about your company's product or industry. Given time, you may be able to educate the agency's people about what you do, but there is no guarantee that they will develop a true feel for your business. Consequently, you could end up wasting thousands of dollars on an ad campaign that misses the mark.
- **Unclear Expectations**: There is always the risk of a disconnect between what you hope to accomplish with the ad campaign and what the agency actually delivers. For the campaign to succeed, you must have a clear objective for what you're trying to accomplish. For example, if you're looking to increase market share by lowering your prices to attract new customers, you need to ensure that an ad campaign highlights your new pricing structure. But an unresponsive agency might offer a different and unsuitable approach.
- **Low Priority:** If you are not regarded as a big client by the ad agency, it may not allocate its best resources to your project. If the agency picks up more big clients after you sign on, you may get pushed even farther down the totem pole. As a result, your project may be assigned to inexperienced staff members.
- **Limited Creative Thinking:** There also is a chance that the agency will take a "one size fits all" approach to your campaign and not take the time to be creative. For example, if the agency developed a successful campaign for a company or product that's similar to yours, or perhaps even did a similar campaign for one or your competitors, it may do the same approach with your product. As a result, the agency may not take into account any changes that have occurred in the marketplace, rendering your campaign obsolete.

Types of Agencies

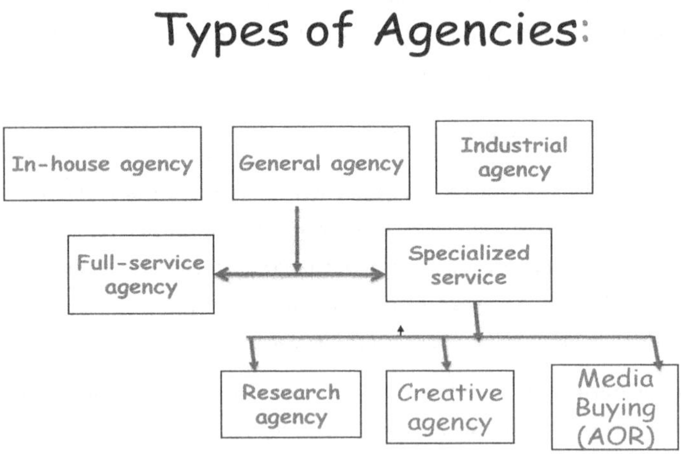

1. **<u>Full-Service Advertising Agency</u>:** A full-service advertising agency is generally a big size advertising agency having all departments, specialized people heading each department and numbers of subordinates under them. It has almost all major departments like – client servicing, account planning, copywriting, art direction, creative studio and production, media planning and buying, accounts etc. All big renowned advertising agencies are generally full-service advertising agencies.

Functions of Full-service Agencies

- Account management
- Creative
- Media planning and placement
- Research

2. **<u>Creative Boutique</u>:** Advertising agencies specialized in creative work are commonly known as creative boutiques. These agencies are not responsible for client handling, campaign strategy plans or media planning; they are solely responsible for the creative idea and its execution. Such agencies are relatively small and have only a few creative people like – copywriters, art directors, and creative heads.

Functions of Creative Boutique

a. Provide Only Creative Services.
b. Full-Service Agencies May Subcontract with Creative Boutiques.
c. Other Functions Provided by the Internal Client Departments.

3. **Media Buying Agency:** Media buying agencies are specialized in media planning, scheduling and buying. Such agencies are also known as agency of record (AOR). These agencies plan and select media, schedule advertisement release dates and time, and then buy media space/time from the publications/television or radio channels. Nowadays full service advertising agencies have a separate media wing, under a separate name, which operates as a media buying agency alone. Such agencies comprise of only media planning and buying specialized people.
4. **Interactive Agency:** Interactive agencies are those advertising agencies which specialize in digital new-age media of advertising communication. Such agencies prepare internet advertisements, sms advertisements, viral advertisements etc. Such advertisements are relatively new, highly interactive, innovative and challenging.
5. **In-house Agency:** Some big companies prefer to have their own in-house advertising agencies. Such in-house agencies solely work for the owner company, and not any other client. These agencies apparently look like any other full-service agency, but they work solely for the owner company. Such agencies are relatively small in terms of manpower. These in-house agencies are responsible for all advertising and marketing communication activities of the company. Many big consumer durable companies have in-house agencies.

Agency Departments

a. **Creative department:** The people who create the actual ads form the core of an advertising agency. Modern advertising agencies usually form their copywriters and art directors into creative teams. Creative teams may be permanent partnerships or formed on a project-by-project basis. The art director and copywriter report to a creative director, usually a creative employee with several years of experience. Although copywriters have the word "write" in their job title, and art directors have the word "art", one does not necessarily write the words and the other draw the pictures; they both generate creative ideas to represent the proposition (the advertisement or campaign's key message). Once they receive the creative brief from their account team, the creative team will concept ideas to take to their creative director for feedback. This can often be a back and forth process, occurring several times before several ads are set to present to the client. Creative departments frequently work with outside design or production studios to develop and implement their ideas. Creative departments may employ production artists as entry-level positions, as well as for operations and maintenance. The creative process forms the most crucial part of the advertising process.

b. **Media services Department:** The *media services* department may not be so well known, but its employees are the people who have contacts with the suppliers of various creative media. For example, they will be able to advise upon and negotiate with printers if an agency is producing flyers for a client. However, when dealing with the major media (broadcast media, outdoor, and the press), this work is usually outsourced to a media agency which can advise on *media planning* and is normally large enough to negotiate prices down further than a single agency or client can. They can often be restrained by the client's budget, in which, the media strategy will inform the creative team what media platform they'll be developing the ad for.

Modern agencies might also have a media planning department integrated, which does all the spot's planning and placements

c. **Production Department:** Without the *production* department, the ads created by the copywriter and art director would be nothing more than words and pictures on paper. The production department, in essence, ensures the TV commercial or print ad, etc., gets produced. They are responsible for contracting external vendors (directors and production companies in the case of TV commercials; photographers and design studios in the case of the print advertising or direct mailers). Producers are involved in every aspect of a project, from the initial creative briefing through execution and delivery. In some agencies, senior producers are known as "executive producers" or "content architects".

d. **Other departments and personnel:** In small agencies, employees may do both creative and account service work. Larger agencies attract people who specialize in one or the other, and indeed include a number of people in specialized positions: production work, Internet advertising, planning, or research, for example.

An often forgotten, but integral, department within an advertising agency is traffic. The traffic department regulates the flow of work in the agency. It is typically headed by a traffic manager (or system administrator). Traffic increases an agency's efficiency and profitability through the reduction of false job starts, inappropriate job initiation, incomplete information sharing, over- and under-cost estimation and the need for media extensions. In small agencies without a dedicated traffic manager, one employee may be responsible for managing workflow, gathering cost estimates and answering the phone, for example. Large agencies may have a traffic department of five or more employees.

Advertising interns are typically university juniors and seniors who are genuinely interested in and have an aptitude for advertising. Internships at advertising agencies most commonly fall into one of five areas of expertise: account services, interactive, media, public relations and traffic. Art students working on the creative side can find internships as an assistant art director or assistant copywriter.

An internship program in account services usually involves fundamental work within account management as well as offering exposure to other facets of the agency. The primary responsibility of this position is to assist account managers. Functions of the account management intern may include:

- Research and analysis: Gathering information regarding industry, competition, customer product or service; as well as presenting findings in verbal/written form with recommendations.
- Involvement in internal meetings and, when appropriate, client meetings.
- Assisting account services in the management of creative projects.

Interns often take part in the internal creative process, where they may be charged with creating and managing a website as well as developing an advertising campaign. Hands on projects such as these help interns learn how strategy and well-developed marketing are essential to a sound advertising and communications plan.

During their internship, the intern will experience the development of an ad, brochure and broadcast or communications project from beginning to end. During the internship, the intern should be exposed to as much as possible within the agency and advertising process.

Methods of Agency Compensation: The different methods of Agency Compensation are as under:

- **Commission Method**: Under this method advertising agency takes there compensation on commission basis. Fee that an advertising agency charges a client for time and effort spent in selecting and supervising production work done by another company (e.g., printing, photoengraving, photography, commercial recording, filming, and film editing). The amount charged the client is usually 17.65% of the gross production cost.
- **Cost-Plus Agreement**: A **cost-plus contract**, also termed a **Cost Reimbursement Contract**, is a contract where a contractor is paid for all of its allowed expenses to a set limit *plus* additional payment to allow for a profit. Cost-reimbursement contracts contrast with fixed-price contract, in which the contractor is paid a negotiated amount regardless of incurred expenses.

- **Percentage Charges**: Percentage-based compensation for contributions is defined as any compensation that is based on a percentage (sometimes referred to as a commission) of contributions raised.
- **Fee Arrangement**: A **Fee Arrangement** or **conditional fee** is any fee for services provided where the fee is payable only if there is a favorable result.
- **Incentive-Based Payment**: Incentive pay, also known as "pay for performance" is generally given for specific performance results rather than simply for time worked. While incentives are *not* the answer to all personnel challenges, they can do much to increase work performance of Advertising Agencies.

How Agencies Gain Clients

- **Referrals**: Referral is a structured and systematic process to maximize word of mouth potential. Referral does this by encouraging, informing, promoting and rewarding customers and contacts to think and talk as much as possible about their supplier, their company, product and service and the value and benefit the supplier brings to them and people they know. Which Increases Client size of Advertising Agency.
- **Solicitations**: *"Solicitation"* means contact by a Advertising agency or advertising agent of a customer for the purpose of selling or offering to sell advertisement services.
- **Presentations**: Where advertising agency used to give more presentation to the various companies about their achievements to the different clients or Companies. With related to their Business, achievements, success etc.
- **Public Relations**: *Using the news or business press to carry positive stories about your company or your products; cultivating a good relationship with local press representatives.*
- **Image, Reputation**: where advertisement agency create there Image and reputation by creating success advertising to their clients. Through which their Image and Reputation become higher.

Why Agencies Lose Clients

- **Poor performance**: Agencies lose their clients when there is poor performance of the agency. Unable to provide creative ads to their Products.
- **Unrealistic Demand:** When Agencies claim huge demand to their clients with related to Payment, remuneration or any other condition this makes agencies to lose their clients.
- **Poor Communication:** when agencies not have an effective communication which leads to loss of clients.

- **Changes in strategies:** If agencies keep on changing their strategies on their functioning and handling of clients it will affect the business.
- **Payment conflict:** when clients are not paying the remuneration or compensation to agency on time also leads to lose of clients.
- **Policy changes:** If ad agency keeps on changing their company policies or payment policies where it also affects ad agency Business.
- **Declining sales:** when the client is not having good sales or decline sales which leads agency to lose their clients.
- **Personality conflict:** when there is no Unity in the agency departments while functioning it also leads to losing client to ad agency.

Top 5 Ad Agencies in India

- Adbur Pvt Ltd.
- Akshara Advertising.
- Mudra Communications Ltd.
- Chaitra Leo Burnett Pvt ltd.
- Crayons Advertising and Marketing Pvt. Ltd.

Top 5 Ad Agencies in the World

Rank	Agency	Headquarters	Revenue (US$ millions)
1	Omnicom Group	New York City	10,481.1
2	WPP Group	LONDON	10,032.2
3	Interpublic Group of Companies	New York City	6,700.0
4	Publicis Groupe	Paris	5,107.2
5	Dentsu*	Tokyo	2,887.8

Examples of Top Advertising Agencies

- **Ogilvy & Mather-** Hutch (Vodafone), Cadbury, Asian Paints and Fevicol.
- **JWT**, J Walter Thompson- Nestle, Bayer, Ford, Nokia and Unilever.
- **Mudra Communication-**Neutrogena, HBO, Philips, Reliance NetConnect, Big Bazaar.
- **FCB Ulka Advertising Ltd-**Tata Indicom, Whirlpool, Zee Cinema, Santoor, Sunfeast and Amul.
- **Grey Worldwide (I) Pvt. Ltd-** Hero Honda, Maruti Suzuki, Nestle, Ambuja Cement, UTV, P&G and Godrej.

Other Types of Agencies

Social Media Agencies

- *Social media* agencies specialize in promotion of brands in the various social media platforms like blogs, social networking sites, Q&A sites, discussion forums, microblogs etc. The two key services of social media agencies are:
  - Social media marketing
  - Online reputation management

Healthcare Communications Agencies

- Healthcare communications agencies specialize in strategic communications and marketing services for the Healthcare and Life Science industries. These agencies distinguish themselves through an understanding of the strict labeling and marketing guidelines mandated by the U.S. Food and Drug Administration (FDA) and industry group guidelines, most notably ADVAMED and PHARMA.

Medical Education Agencies

- Medical education agencies specialize in creating educational content for the Healthcare and Life Science industries. These agencies typically specialize in one of two areas:
- Promotional education - education and training materials tied to the promotion of a given product or therapy.
- Continuing medical education - accredited education and training materials created for continuing physician and medical professional education.

CHAPTER V

Advertising Budget & Regulation

Topics: Advertising Plans, Process, different methods, sales objectives and task all you can afford comparative parity and incremental concept; budgeting decisions rules, Ethical and social dimension of advertising, Role of computer in advertising.

- Topics: Advertisement regulations, deceptive advertising, determining deceptive advertising research, remedies, competitors, lawsuits, self regulations, advertising and society.
- Effects on values and lifestyles, economic effects of advertising, advertising and competition.

What is advertising Budget?

- An estimation of a company's promotional expenditures over a period of time. An advertising budget is the money a company is willing to set aside to accomplish its marketing objectives. When creating the advertising budget, a company must weigh the trade-offs between spending one additional advertising dollar with the amount of revenue that dollar will bring in as revenue.

Consideration of Advertising Budget

- Developing advertising Budget requires two basic considerations:
  a. The budget must be constructed within the financial capabilities of the company and
  b. The Budget must contain specific details on the allocation of funds to specific operations.

Factors influencing Advertising Budget

a. **The Product stage in Product life cycle**: The Products newly introduced must be heavily advertised to create market awareness. This necessitates heavy promotional expenditure with little expected profits.

b. **Competitor's strategy**: advertising strategy and advertising budget is directly influenced by the competitors strategy. If the competitors are advertising heavily, then a higher budget would be needed to neutralise the competitors edge in market and maintain its own market share.

c. **Quality of campaign**: If the message is creative, high impacting leaving and effective in customer persuasion even a small budget will be equally effective.

d. **The Budget Period**: Budget appropriations would also depend upon the time period for which the budget is prepared. For example a budgeting cycle of 2-4 months offers greater degree of flexibility in coping with changing environment.

e. **Affordability:** The advertising budget should be within the capability of the advertiser to bear. However, where advertiser feels the the campaign is very promising and potential. An adventurous management may take a risk of spending heavily even beyond its affordability.

f. **Contingency Planning:** some contingency funds must be kept aside to meet certain unexpected developments both in internal and external environment. Example: change in competitors strategy, change in law applicable to the product/media/message etc.

Problems in Advertising Budget

a. The effects of external variables such as population or income, changes in economic conditions and competitive behavior.

b. Variations in the quality of advertising

c. Uncertainties as to the time- lag effect of advertising.

d. The effect of the firm's other marketing activities such as product improvement and stepped up personal selling.

Advertising Budget Process: The actual budgetary Process consists of following four steps:

a. **Preparation of the Budget**: The advertising budget is prepared by the marketing manger usually for a year. The total budget is then segmented into different markets, time periods and geographical areas. The advertising budget is based on the data collected by marketing research agencies and it primarily relates to following:
   - The type of product to be advertised.
   - Whether product is newly introduced or an established one.
   - The targeted audience and its demographic composition.
   - Advertising copy and media selection.

b. **Presentation and approval of the Budget:** The Budget so developed by the marketing manager is then presented before an executive committee or a financial committee. The committee than objectively analyzes the budget presented and gives its recommendations. It is finally approved by vice president of marketing or the Chief Executive officer of the firm.

c. **Execution of the Budget:** After the budget has been approved. Channels and media for budget allocation have been considered, the task of preparing advertising message and acquiring time and space is given to the advertising agency.

d. **Control of Budget:** Advertising manager also ensures that the allocated funds are used for advertising and no other purpose. He has to ensure that no advertising fund is utilised for other promotional techniques like personal selling, Public relations etc.

Methods of Advertising Budget: There are several allocation methods used in developing a budget. The most common are listed below:

a. **PERCENTAGE OF SALES METHOD** Due to its simplicity, the percentage of sales method is the most commonly used by small businesses. When using this method an advertiser takes a percentage of either past or anticipated sales and allocates that percentage of the overall budget to advertising. Critics of this method, though, charge that using past sales for figuring the advertising budget is too conservative and that it can stunt growth.

b. **OBJECTIVE AND TASK METHOD** Because of the importance of objectives in business, the task and objective method is considered by many to make the most sense, and is therefore used by most large businesses.

c. **COMPETITIVE PARITY METHOD** While keeping one's own objectives in mind, it is often useful for a business to compare its advertising spending with that of its competitors. The theory here is that if a business is aware of how much its competitors are spending to inform, persuade, and remind (the three general aims of advertising) the consumer of their products and services, then that business can, in order to remain competitive, either spend more, the same, or less on its own advertising.

d. **MARKET SHARE METHOD** Similar to competitive parity, the market share method bases its budgeting strategy on external market trends. With this method a business equates its market share with its advertising expenditures

e. **UNIT SALES METHOD** This method takes the cost of advertising an individual item and multiplies it by the n

f. **ALL AVAILABLE FUNDS METHOD** This aggressive method involves the allocation of all available profits to advertising purposes. This can be risky for a business of any size; for it means that no money is being used to help the business grow in other ways (purchasing new technologies, expanding the work force, etc.).? Number of units the advertiser wishes to sell.

g. **AFFORDABLE METHOD:** With this method, advertisers bases their budgets on what they can afford. Of course, arriving at a conclusion about what a small business can afford in the realm of advertising is often a difficult task, one that needs to incorporate overall objectives and goals, competition, presence in the market, unit sales, sales trends, operating costs, and other factors

Social Dimension in Advertising

a. **Cultural and value Issues:** Advertisements' must cope with culture environment and value systems of the society. Otherwise they will not be acceptable for the society and they will be opposed and create adverse impact on the promotion objectives.
b. **Standard of Living:** Advertisements enhance the standard of living of the society by providing the information about new and innovation products for use. To make life comfortable smart and easy. But at the same time it is criticized on the basis that society is forced by advertisement to purchase something beyond their limits as status symbols and it creates disturbance and extra burden for people.
c. **Knowledge to society:** Advertisements provide knowledge to the society about the products and services produced and distributed about the different business organization. The decision making of an individual becomes sharp in presence of adequate options.
d. **Society Government Chain:** advertisements work as a chain between government and society and the policies and issues concerned with welfare and development are communicated by government by the help of advertisement.

It is generally agreed that advertising exerts a powerful social influence and is criticized for encouraging materialism in society. It is also blamed for manipulating consumers to buy things for which they have no real need, depicting stereotypes and controlling the media.

Ethical Dimensions of Advertisements

- Good ethics can be good business. When you place advertisements for your small business, it can be tempting to bend the truth about your company, products or services, but that approach can be short-sighted.
- The gain that may come from stretching the truth can become a loss as customers come to distrust your company for using deceptive advertising. Examine the areas where you can be held accountable for the ethical aspects of your advertising.
    a. **Psychoactive Ads:** Psychoactive advertising is any commercial message that has a detrimental emotional impact on the target audience. This can include anxiety, low self-esteem and hostility. If these emotions become intense enough, harm can be

done to the viewer. These types of ads are not illegal, but they may be seen as unethical because of the emotional pain they inflict.

b. **Deception Ads:** Lying about a product's features or benefits is illegal as well as unethical. Your small business can lose its reputation quickly by engaging in this practice. In addition, misleading your customer about your business history or longevity is an unethical advertising practice. When you start a business, you may be anxious to appear solid and reliable, but deceiving the public about your track record will make you seem unreliable.

c. **Using Stereotypes:** Using racial and sexual stereotypes raises ethical questions. Not only do they portray certain groups in a negative light, they portray the advertiser in a negative light. These kinds of messages can cause a media outlet to stop accepting advertising from you and harm your reputation in the community. In addition, stereotypes about the handicapped, teenagers and groups such as executives or laborers, though common, cast your small business in a bad light.

d. **Targeting Children:** Many products and services are legitimately for children. Advertisements that make a straightforward pitch of these types of products to kids can be legitimate. The murky issues arise when an advertiser promotes items that are illegal or unhealthy (such as cigarettes, alcohol and fatty foods) to children. The illegal products can land an advertiser in court; the unhealthy ones can cause an advertiser to be tried and found guilty in the court of public opinion. In addition, ads aimed at kids should not contain sexuality and adult themes.

e. **Sexuality in Advertising:** Sex has been used to sell products for a long time. You are not violating ethical rules when you place an attractive female in an advertisement. However, the continuous portrayal of women as sex objects and men as mindless pursuers of females can make your small business look unsavory. Also, the gratuitous use of sexual images that have nothing to do with your pitch or your product can cause some customers to turn away from your business for fear you are manipulating them.

Role of Computer in Advertising

Marketing is the process by which goods are sold and purchased. The aim of marketing is to acquire, retain, and satisfy customers. Modern marketing has evolved into a complex and diverse field. In today's extremely competitive business environment businesses are searching for ways to improve profitability and to maintain their position in the marketplace. As competition becomes more intense the formula for success becomes more difficult. One particular thing has greatly aided companies in their quests to accomplish these goals and that is the computer. Some of the roles computers play in these changing marketing trends is as follows.

One role of computers in marketing is inventory control. Computers are now used to keep records of inventory. Inventory keeping allows Inventory control systems maintain information about activities within firms that ensure the delivery of products to customers. The subsystems that perform these functions include sales, manufacturing, warehousing, ordering, and receiving.

Benefits of Using Computer in Advertising

The advantages of using computer in advertising is so far exceed that of traditional print publication through costs, availability, wider consumer markets, and the potential for increased profit margins. Considering that traditional print methods and distribution are tried and true, the technological trends of the Internet surpass it at each level of the marketing process. In evaluating this statement, consider the following in each of the aforementioned areas.

To better understand the differences, some clarity in the two advertising mediums must be identified. Traditional print advertising is composed of common marketing collateral. Most of us better define this collateral as brochures, pamphlets, newspaper advertisements, billboards, business cards, and the like. Internet advertising is the conglomeration of electronics-a computer, or server, residing of the same marketing collateral on a professionally designed website, which is also better known as an electronic storefront. Lastly, a promotion, or campaign can be illustrated in the perspective of a "buy one, get one free" or "twenty-percent off, this week only" sales, and the process each business must adhere to, in distributing that information out to the consumer.

In evaluating costs in traditional print publication, hefty expenses are incurred through ad design for each campaign or promotion, printing fees, and storage facilities to house the boxes and bundles of material. Further, there is the distribution cost to analyze; the costs of labor to compile the marketing material, transportation to deliver the quantities of print material, and of course, the postage itself. When these expenses are applied to television and radio media, the costs may soar into five and six figure domains. If a traditionally printed promotion requires an error modification, it may incur nearly all of the costs to be paid, yet a second time, even for something as simple proofreader's oversight. To illustrate this point, open any newspaper or magazine, and inspect them closely-both actually have sections specifically for corrections.

In contrast, while the initial startup costs of an Internet website may be at times comparable to that of a one-time promotion in traditional print media, the costs are considerably lower for the following reasons; there is no postage to affix, no expense bared for storage, delivery, or repeated design fees for each new promotion. The Internet website is reusable, recyclable, and rarely falls into redundancy with outdated material. Monthly fees are minimal for site hosting (the location of the actual website). When considering the advantages of Internet-based advertising, the error modification incurs little to no costs to repair typographical errors and wrong promotion dates. It's much easier to fix an oversight like this at the spur of the moment, and often only takes a moment!

In addressing availability of a business, traditional print promotions are time-centered. The hours of a business or service are limited to the hours they are physically open, thereby limiting potential sales to consumers during the "off-hours." Additionally, the promotion is viable for a set period of time, and upon the expiration of that set period, the costs are again presented in repeating the same process for each individual promotion.

Whereas the availability of an Internet website allows consumer access to information, and more importantly access to sales twenty-four hours per day, seven days per week, throughout the entire year. This is also known as "24x7x365" availability. Furthermore, each promotion may not necessarily incur additional costs, requiring only a minor modification of dollar amounts, numbers, and verbiage for products and/or services in a short few minutes, as opposed to redesigning an entire promotion in traditional print with immediate access available to the public.

In weighing the advantages of Internet versus traditional print methods, the consumer market potential is extremely limited in the traditional venue with geographical restrictions in most media being available only to the local viewing area, and when larger budgets allow-national markets can be approached. Rarely can a small-mid-size business approach sales on a national, or global level.

By comparison, the Internet is an extreme opposite, having no physical or geographical limitations, and broadening the consumer base on the massive global scale. There is no cost associated with reaching and opening up the potential for consumers across the globe. The website is readily available to any consumer with a computer, and in this day and age, includes the majority of consumers throughout the world. There are no additional costs in reaching the expanded global markets.

Finally, the overall picture can be viewed in financial terms, or specifically, the profit margin. For each dollar that is spent in advertising, a business will take for granted, it will acquire a potential, paying customer. For comparison purposes, let us imagine, a business with a failed or badly timed promotion has incurred the costs of the traditional print media and expended much time and money into the profit per customer at the higher costs, while the Internet advertiser has a similar promotion, incurring little to no additional costs. This can be equated in dollars and common sense. For the traditional advertiser, it may seem like little with two dollars expended to reach a new customer, but not nearly as impressive as the dime or quarter it required for the Internet advertiser to reach an infinite number of potential customers.

The bottom line is that the advantages of Internet advertising do far exceed that of it's traditional print predecessor, as reflected in the lessened costs, the '24x7x365' availability, the expanded consumer markets, and predominantly in the overall profit margin per each consumer.

Meaning

Advertising regulation refers to the laws and rules defining the ways in which products can be advertised in a particular region. Rules can define a wide number of different aspects, such as placement, timing, and content. In the United States, false advertising and health-related ads are regulated the most.

Advertising Industry in India is on the expansion spree for the last few years and has become a serious and big business growing at a considerable rate. However, the growth of this industry is affected by the prevalent malpractices carried out by advertisers in order to lure the consumers and sustaining an edge over the competitors. Advertisement is often described as commercial speech and enjoys protection under Article 19(1)(a) of the Indian Constitution. As a facet of the Right to Information, it facilitates the dissemination of information about the sellers and their products. However, the manner of facilitation is subject to a number of statutory provisions.

Under the Indian legal regime, the prominent, prohibitory legal provisions that regulate advertising are:

- Obscene publication or advertisement of a lottery under the Indian Penal Code.
- Harmful publication under the Young Persons (Harmful Publications) Act, 1956.
- The indecent representation of women under the Indecent Representation of Women (Prohibition) Act, 1986.
- Use of report of test or analysis for advertising any drug or cosmetic under the Drugs and Cosmetics Act, 1940.
- Inviting transplantation of organs under the Transplantation of Human Organs Act, 1994.

- Advertisement of magical remedies of diseases and disorders under Drugs and Magical Remedies (Objectionable Advertisements) Act, 1954.
- Advertisements relating to prenatal determination of sex uner the Prenatal Diagnostic Techniques (Regulation and Prevention of Misuse) Act, 1994.
- Advertisements of cigarettes and other tobacco products under tah Cigarettes and other Tobacco Products (Prohibition of Advertisement and Regulation of Trade and Commerce, Production, Supply and Distribution) Act, 2003.
- Any political advertisement forty hours prior to polling time under the Representation of People Act, 1951.

Why does Advertising Need to be Regulated?

Advertising plays an essential part in all market economies. It stimulates growth and innovation, encourages competition and increases consumer choice. It is a swift and efficient means of making consumers aware of product innovations and keeping them informed of the range, nature and quality of the products available to them. Advertising is an important element in maintaining or increasing market share and vital to the introduction of a new product or the improvement of an existing one.

To fulfill this important task, advertising must enjoy a high level of consumer trust and confidence; it must be legal, decent, honest and truthful. If consumers are misled by advertising, they will not buy again; if it offends them, they will not buy in the first place. Bad advertising, even though it may account for only a small percentage of the whole, will gradually undermine consumer confidence and all advertising will suffer. So it is in the interests of the advertising industry to ensure that advertising is properly regulated. Traditionally, there have been two ways of doing this; one is detailed legislation, the other is called self-regulation.

What are the Benefits of Self-regulation?

FOR CONSUMERS: By avoiding the complexities and delays of a judicial process, self-regulation offers consumers a quick, uncomplicated, easily-accessible and (because it is funded by the advertising industry) often cost-free means of having their complaints handled. Self-regulation is also flexible enough to adapt to changing societal views as well as advertising media / techniques. It can apply immediate sanctions by publishing the jury decisions and by pushing for media refusal or withdrawal of advertisements.

FOR ADVERTISING INDUSTRY: Having effective self-regulation in place means that the advertising industry pro-actively makes sure its advertising messages are honest, decent, truthful and legal. This will allow the advertising industry to build up a strong trust relationship with the consumer, thus promoting further consumption of the products and services advertised.

Self-regulation is also an alternative to detailed legislation, but not to all legislation. It is now widely accepted that self-regulation works best within a legislative framework. The two complement each other, like the frame and strings of a tennis racquet, to produce a result which neither could achieve on its own. The law lays down broad principles, e.g. that advertising should not be misleading, while self-regulatory codes, because of their greater flexibility and the fact that they are interpreted in spirit as well as the letter, can deal quickly and efficiently with the detail of individual advertisements. Framework legislation therefore creates a legal backstop which self-regulation will need to invoke when dealing with fraudulent and/or illegal practices (like for example pornography) as well as rogue traders – those operators who repeatedly refuse to abide by any laws.

How is Self-regulation Achieved & Who Applies the Self-regulation Rules?

The advertising industry draws up a code of standards and practice, which it formally agrees to support, financially, morally and practically. Then it sets up a body to apply the code and ensures that it is properly staffed and funded. This body is called a Self-Regulatory Organisation - SRO for short. The aim is to keep advertising standards high and ensure consumer trust and protection to the benefit to all.

Advertising council of India: Regulating body of advertising in India.

- Advertising Standards Council of India is a self regulatory voluntary organization of the advertising industry.
- In recent years the quantity of false, misleading and offensive advertising has resulted in consumers having an increasing disbelief in advertising, and a growing resentment of it. Misleading, false advertising also constitutes unfair competition.
- SELF REGULATION GETS LEGAL RECOGNITION.
- ASCI CODE MADE COMPULSORY FOR TV ADS.
- Self-Regulation in advertising as practiced and duly recognized in many countries including USA, UK,

Australia, Japan, China and Brazil etc., has been pursued and monitored in India in an inexpensive and expeditious manner for the last 20 years by the Advertising Standards Council of India (ASCI), a voluntary and non-profit organization set up by a group of advertisers, advertising agencies, media etc., way back in 1985, with the objective of ensuring that all advertising should be legal, decent, honest and truthful along with a sense of social responsibility to the consumer and to the rules of fair competition.

Deceptive Advertising: Advertising that makes false claims or misleading statements, as well as advertising that creates a false impression. If retailers systematically advertise merchandise at low prices to get customers into their stores and then fail to have the merchandise, they are guilty of deceptive advertising.

Deceptive practices can take many other forms as well, such as false promises, unsubstantiated claims, incomplete descriptions, false testimonials or comparisons, small-print qualifications of advertisements, partial disclosure, or visual distortion of products. Anyone-including the manufacturer of a product, the advertising agency preparing the advertisement, the retailer, or even a celebrity who endorses a product-can be prosecuted for making unsubstantiated claims about a product or service.

As a matter of fact, any advertising that leads the consumer to make purchase decisions based on false assumptions about the price and quality of competitive products is considered deceptive practice and is punishable by law. Responsibility for enforcement of the laws dealing with unfair and deceptive advertising comes under the jurisdiction of the federal trade commission.

Definition Deceptive Advertising

The FTC defines this as being a representation, omission, act or practice that is likely to mislead consumers acting reasonably under the circumstances. To be regulated, however, a deceptive claim must also be material.

Misrepresentation or Omission

There are a variety of ways in which misrepresentation or omissions can occur:

- Suggesting that a small difference is important.
- Artificial product demonstration.
- Using an ambiguous or easily confused phrase.
- Implying a benefit that does not fully or partially exist.
- Incorrectly implying that an endorser uses and advocates the brand.
- Omitting a needed qualification.
- Marking a claim without substantiation.

Remedies: The FTC has a variety of remedies at its disposal and must select the remedies most appropriate to the situation. Among the remedies are the ceases and desist order, restitution, affirmative disclosure, and corrective advertising.

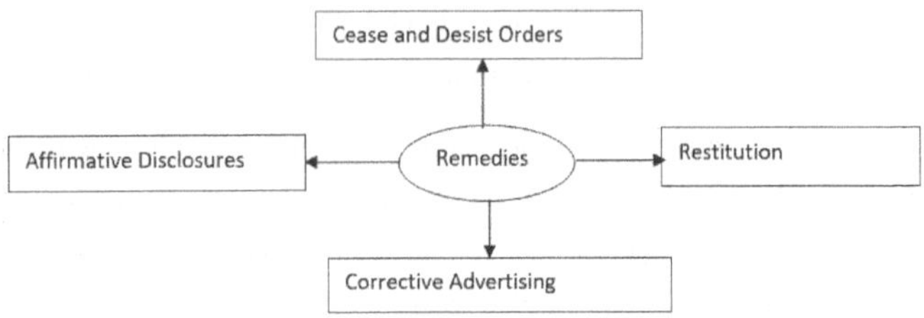

- **Cease-and-Desist Orders**: The cease-and desist order, which prohibits the respondent from engaging further in the deceptive practice, is actually the only formal procedure established by the FTC Act for enforcing its prohibition of "deceptive acts and practices". It has been critized as being a command to "go and sin no more", which has little practical effect.
- **Restitution:** Restitution means that the consumer is compensated for any damage. For example, the FTC required a mail order company to make restitution in the form of full refunds for its skin cream, diet plans, vitamin supplements, and other products that had advertised claims not adequately substantiated. Restitution is rarely considered because of its severity.
- **Affirmative Disclosures**: If an advertisement has provided insufficient information to the consumer, an affirmative disclosure might be issued. Affirmative disclosures require "clear and conspicuous" disclosure of the omitted information. Often the involved information relates to deficiencies or limitations of the product or service relating to matters of health or safety.
- **Corrective advertising**: Corrective advertising requires advertisers to rectify past deception by making suitable statement in future commercials.

Competitors Lawsuits

Another mechanism that inhibits deceptive advertising is the possibility of competitor lawsuits. In which firms charge that false advertising has caused them damage. In one case, a suit was successfully brought by Honeywell against a competitor who supplied replacement parts to Honeywell's safety control systems and had incorrectly claimed that its products had comparable quality and ease of replacement to that of Honeywell.

During the last decade, the 1946 Lauham Trademark Act has been broadened to provide the basic for suits in which a competitor has been disparaged in a comparative ad. In one visible case, an automatic rental firm Jartran, ran a series of ads that were judged to have damaged U-Haul. In one ad, a special introductory Jartran price was compared to U-Haul's usual price, implying a price difference that did not exist. In another, older, smaller U-Haul trucks were compared to new larger Jartran trucks, incorrectly implying a difference between the average trucks in the two fleets.

In most cases, the relief is an injunction to stop the offending practice. However, a wide range of remedies exit. In the Jartran case, the firm was ordered to replace $6 million in lost U-Haul profits and another $13.6 million to compensate for U-Hauls corrective advertising outlay. Another $20 million was assessed because the action was judged to be willful and malicious.

Self Regulations

A self regulation is another vehicle to combat deceptive advertising by national advertisers in place in the United States since 1971. It is intended to provide a fact, flexible alternative to FTC and the courts. Complaints from consumers or competitors are investigated by the National Advertising Division (NAD), an arm of the council of Better Business Bureaus (CBBB). In evaluating a complaint, NAD normally requests that the advertisers substantiation for the claims made in the challenged advertisements. If the complaint is judged to be justified and substantiation found to be inadequate, the advertiser is requested to modify or withdraw the challenged advertising. The finding can be appealed to a panel drawn mostly from the advertising industry.

The self regulation process does provide remedies in a meaningful number of cases perhaps 100 cases each year are brought before the NAD. Although the penalties are relatively minor a case can generate negative publicity, or bring in the FTC, or suggest to major media that they deny access to the offender-as a practical matter, nearly all advertisers comply with NAD findings. The biggest value, however, is probably to provide a forum to establish standards for advertisers and to make visible issues regarding deception in advertising.

Advertising and Society: Effects on Values and Lifestyles

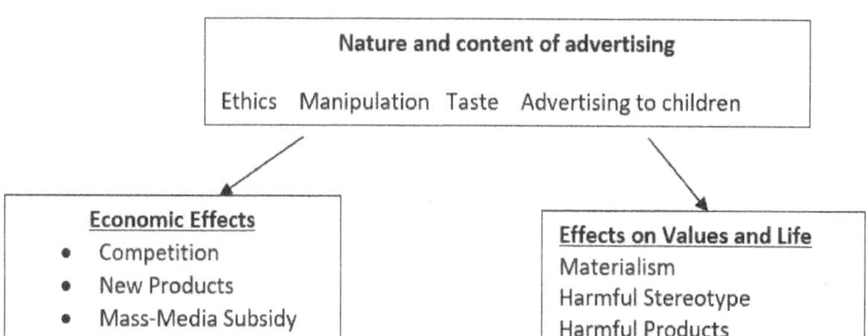

- **Ethics**: Ethics is it ethical to advertise cigarettes or to engage in alcohol advertising which might persuade young people to start smoking or drinking? These and other questions of advertising and marketing ethics have become subjects of heated debate in recent years.
- **Emotional Appeals**: The communication of factual information about a product's primary function is usually accepted as being of value to the consumer. However, when advertising utilizes appeals or associations that go beyond such a basic communication task, the charge of manipulation via emotional appeals is raised.

First, banning television advertising to protect those children who donot understand the selling intent of commercials will deny advertisers the right of free speech to communicate with other audience members, who in fact constitute the great majority of the audience for most children's programme.

- **Effects on values and Lifestyle**: Advertising by its very nature receives wide exposure. Further more it presumably has an effect on what people buy and thus on their activities. Because of this exposure and because of its roles as a persuasive vehicle, it is argued that it has an impact on the values and lifestyles of society and that this impact has its negative as well as positive side.

The key issues are which values and lifestyles are be encouraged as healthy, which are to be avoided, and what relative impact or influence advertising has on them. Despite their difficulty and their relationship to deep philosophical questions, they are well worth addressing to illuminate judgments and assumptions about our market system and society that are too often glossed over.

- **Materialism**: materialism is defined as the tendency to give undue importance to material interests. Presumably, there is a corresponding lessening of importance to non material interests such as love, freedom and intellectual pursuits.
- **Promoting stereotypes**: The accusation that advertising has contributed to the role stereo typing of women and ethic minorities has been supported by several studies. In 729 advertisements appearing in 1970, non showed women in a professional capacity, whereas 35 of them so portrayed men. The authors concluded that the advertisements reflected the stereo-types that women do not do important things, are dependent on men, are regarded by men primarily as sex objects, and should be in the home.

Economic Effects of Advertising

It is unreasonable to separate the economic and social impact of advertising. The social issues, by themselves, tend to focus on the negative aspects of advertising- its intrusiveness, content that is in bad taste, and the possibly undesirable impact on values and lifestyles. If advertising were regarded solely on these grounds, it would be difficult to defend, despite the fact that much advertising is entertaining, some may even be of real artistic value, and some is directed toward supporting causes that are universally praised. Advertising is basically an economic institution. It performs an economic function for an advertiser, affects economic decisions of the audience, and is an integral part of the whole economic system. Thus, an economic evaluation should accompany other types of appraisal of advertising. Here are some of the economic benefits of advertising:

a. Advertising provides informational utility
b. Maintains or enhances brand equity.
c. Supports the media
d. Provides employment
e. Reduces distribution costs.
f. Provides product utility.
g. Stimulates introduction of new products.

Advertising and Competition

The existence of vigorous competition is important to a market economy. Competitive forces lead to real product innovation, the efficient distribution of goods, and the absence of inflated prices. The question is what impact does advertising have on competition? There have been hypotheses put forth indicating that advertising can actually decrease the level of competition. For example, it is argued that heavy advertising expenditures in many industries generate strong brand loyalty that tends to create barriers to potential competitors. The hypotythesized result is fewer competitors, less competition, and higher prices.

One measure of competition within an industry is the degree to which the sales of the industry are concentrated in the hands of few firms. The specific construct is the concentration ratio: that is, the share of industry sales held by the competition is theorized to be less vigorous and high prices results. Among many industries that would qualify under this criterion are automobiles, aircraft, electric lamps, flat glass, primary aluminum, and household refrigerators and freezers.

CHAPTER VI

Advertising & Media Management

- Role of Media, Setting Media Budget
- Types of media
- Media Research and Advertising Decisions
- Media vehicles Decision
- Media option decisions, scheduling and timing decisions
- Media buying and organization

Advertising

- Paid non personal communication about an organization and its products transmitted to a target audience through mass media.
- Promotes goods, services, ideas, images, issues, people, and anything else that advertisers want to publicize or foster.

Why Do We Do Advertising?

- Personal Selling is preferred, because it is so effective - but, it is expensive sometimes to contact EVERYBODY this way.
- Advertising is not as direct as Personal Selling, but you can reach a lot of people.

Advertising Objectives

- Specific Communication Tasks.
- Accomplished with a Specific Target Audience.
- During a Specific Period of Time.
- INFORMATIVE ADVERTISING – builds PRIMARY Demand.
- PERSUASIVE ADVERTISING – builds SELECTIVE Demand.
- COMPARISON ADVERTISING – compares one brand to another.
- REMINDER ADVERTISING – keeps consumers thinking about product.

Media Defined

- The vehicles that carry the ads to the target market.
- Which is most important? Picking the correct media or having great creative?
- What are the types of media?

What is Media?

- In **general,** "media" refers to various means of communication. For example, television, radio, and the newspaper are different types of media.
- In the **computer world**, "media" is also used as a collective noun, but refers to different types of data storage options.

Organization of the Media Function

- Media planner
- Media buyer
- Media researcher

Role of Media in Advertising

1. The basic purpose of advertising is to make the information reach to maximum people and thus help in not only market expansion and leadership but also in making products services or systems to be popularized and known.
2. It works as a profitability indicator and the feedback received helps in further decision making, forecasting and in making business strategies for future promotion.
3. Media helps in gaining and retaining attention of people as prospective customers.
4. It serves as a Global tool for accessing people throughout the globe and making the chances of profitability fast and minimizes the risk factor.
5. Advertising can be initiated in different forms the main channels include radio, television, journals, newspaper, direct mail, billboard, yellow pages, transit space, poster, directories etc.

What Is a Media Budget?

Typical media budgets include funds for online, print and broadcast advertising; interactive social media; consultants' fees; brochures, booklets or videos; equipment or software required to produce company media; and all production costs related to media content creation.

How Media Budgets are Set?

Media budgets are generally established in one of four ways.

1. First, a budget may be set when an owner or executive arbitrarily chooses a figure that constitutes media spending for the year.
2. Second, a media budget may be pegged to a company's sales, with a certain percentage of sales dedicated to media spending.

3. Third, media spending may be based on the amount of money spent on media by competing businesses.
4. Finally, a media budget may be determined by making reasonable assumptions from data about what will be required to reach the desired market or sales results.

Who Controls the Media Budget?

- In smaller companies, media budgets are under the control of the company's owner or CEO, who generally oversees every part of the company's budget and approves all major purchases.
- In larger companies with marketing departments, the media budget may be controlled by a media or advertising director, or by a vice-president of marketing or advertising Department.

Media Budget Factors that MUST BE CONSIDERED

- Market Share & Consumer Base
- Competition & Clutter
- Advertising Frequency
- Product Substitutability
- Stage in the PLC (Product Life Cycle)

Methods of Advertising/Media Budgets

1. **The Percent of Sales Method:** The advertising campaign budget is a constant percentage of desired sales. A car manufacturer may spend less than 1% of sales.
2. This method works as long as the advertising campaign budget is set as a percentage of desired sales.
3. **The Task Objective Method:** How much money do you need to spend to reach the specific goals you have outlined for the advertising campaign? This is especially effective when you are starting out, or if you are trying to grow rapidly.
4. **The Historical Method:** How much did you spend to reach your sales goals in previous years or periods? You will find that by tracking your ads, you will know in advance what you need to do to accomplish your goals.
5. **Competitive Parity:** With competitive parity you spend in equal amounts to your competitors as a percentage of market share. This is a self-defense method of budgeting marketing and advertising expenditures.

6. **Share of Market - Share of Voice:** This method links market share to advertising expenditure. A company with a 20% market share would spend slightly more than 20% of the total advertising dollars spent in the market for that product or service.
7. **The Combination Method:** The best advertising campaign budget you can set will be based on some combination of all of the previous models. You want to maintain a minimum level of advertising, fulfill specific goals, maintain your market share, keep up with your competitors, and compare everything to last year.

What is Media Research?

- It is to do with the most efficient media selection and the evaluation of the advertising media effectiveness both before and after the selection of media schedule.
- Media Research is undertaken to select most suitable media for carrying the advertisers' message to the targeted audience.
- It aims at finding out both 'reach' and 'impact'.
- Reach means coverage and impact means the impression created by a medium on the people.

Role of Media Research

- It helps the advertiser should select the right media.
- It helps the advertiser to stay within advertising budgets.
- It evaluates advertising effectiveness.

Media Terminology

- **Media Planning** - A series of decisions involving the delivery of messages to audiences.
- **Media Objectives** - Goals to be attained by the media strategy and program.
- **Media Strategy** - Decisions on how the media objectives can be attained – indicative of the media budget.
- **Media** - The various categories of delivery systems, including broadcast and print media.
- **Broadcast Media** - Either radio or television network.
- **Print Media** - Publications such as newspapers and magazines.
- **Media Vehicle** - The specific message carrier, such as the Times of India, Femina, KBC, MTV Roadies.
- **Coverage** - The potential audience that might receive the message through the vehicle.
- **Reach** - The actual number of individual audience members reached at least once by the vehicle in a given period of time.
- **Frequency** - The number of times the receiver is exposed to vehicle in a specific time period.

Key Media Terms

- **Media plan**: document that establishes how media will be used to disseminate an advertiser's message, including objectives and strategy.
- **Media objective**: statement in media plan that explains the goals of the plan; usually states how many of the target will be exposed to advertising messages in a given time period, and how often.
- **Media strategy**: statement in media plan that outlines how objectives will be accomplished; shows where and when advertising messages will appear, and at what cost.

Types of Media Used in Advertising

- The types of media used in Advertising can be broadly classified into:
  a. **Traditional or Mass Media:** TV, Radio. Idea to reach large audience.
  b. **Niche Media:** Cable TV, Direct mail, etc. Reach the target audience with specific demographics, narrowly defined target audience.
  c. **Non-Conventional Media:** Internet.

Newspapers - largest share of advertising, 26%

Magazines - 12%

Television - 2nd major category, 14%

Radio - 7%

Direct Mail

Outdoor, billboards etc. - 6%

Types of Media and there Characteristics are as under:

a. Television Characteristics

Advantages	**Disadvantages**
• Mass coverage	• Low selectivity
• High reach	• Short message life
• Impact of sight, sound, and motion	• High absolute cost
• High prestige	• High production costs
• Low cost per exposure	• Clutter
• Attention getting	• Fleeting message
• Favorable image	

b. Radio Characteristics

Advantages	*Disadvantages*
• Local coverage • Low cost • High frequency • Flexible • Low production costs • Well-segmented audiences	• Audio only • Clutter • Low attention getting • Fleeting message

c. Newspapers Characteristics

Advantages	*Disadvantages*
• High coverage • Low cost • Short lead time for placing ads • Ads can placed in interest sections • Timely (current ads) • Reader controls exposure • Can be used for coupons	• Short life • Clutter • Low attention-getting capabilities • Poor reproduction quality • Selective reader exposure

d. Outdoor Characteristics

Advantages	*Disadvantages*
• Location specific • High resolution • Easily noticed	• Short exposure time requires short ad • Poor image • Local restrictions

e. Magazine characteristics

Advantages	*Disadvantages*
• Segmentation potential • Quality reproduction • High information content • Longevity • Multiple readers – pass-on-readership	• Long lead time for ad placement • Visual only • Lack of flexibility

f. Direct Mail Characteristics

Advantages	*Disadvantages*
• High selectivity • Reader controls exposure • High information content • Opportunities for repeat exposures	• High cost/contact • Poor image (junk mail) • Clutter

g. Internet / Interactive Media Characteristics

Advantages	*Disadvantages*
• User selects product information • User attention and involvement • Interactive relationship • Direct selling potential • Flexible message platform	• Limited creative capabilities • Web snarl (crowded access) • Technology limitations • Few valid measurement techniques • Limited reach

Factors Influencing Selection of Media

1. Target Market: Before assessing and evaluating the various media available, the advertiser has to study in detail the firm's target Audience. It is essential that advertiser to studies and understands the characteristics of target customers. Example: Advertise for expensive perfumes and dresses in women's magazine like Famina.
2. Advertising Objectives: the choice of media also depends on the marketing objectives of the company because ultimately the advertising campaign has to be directed towards attaining these objectives.
3. Advertising Budget: No company has unlimited budget for advertising a company should try to maximize the target market.

Example: Advertising in newspapers and magazines also gives wide coverage with comparatively low cost.

4. Product itself and the Medium: the characteristics of the product itself influence the choice of media. If the product is such which requires demonstration of utility then a T.V commercial is more suitable.

Example: Fully automatic washing machines, imported perfumes and Diamond Jewellery require advertisement in high class magazines printed on glossy Papers.

5. Advertising by competitors: Like few company might select the same media as its competitors to enable consumers compare and choose. Advertisers think that his

competitors have chosen wrong media for advertising or they have better option to advertise.

6. Media Penetration and Media coverage: Penetration is defined as the size of audience that is claimed by a media where 80% of population has TV sets of their homes, and then TV penetration is 80%.
7. Quality of Media: Quality of media especially in case of print media also determines the quality of message. A magazine of good quality is better medium than one with poor quality paper such as newspaper.
8. Restrictions and flexibility of media
9. Trade acceptance: Degree of acceptance that a medium can generate among the advertisers intermediaries such as wholesalers and retailers would generate more favorable effect.

Example: Advertisement placed in trade journal which is popular among intermediaries will have positive effect.

Advertising/Media Scheduling

- Media Scheduling means the programming of media insertions or actual placements of advertisements as per time schedule.
- This is the task of physical run of events through press, TV, cinema, radio and promotional media.

Factors Specifying Media Scheduling

- Media category: It specifies the type of media selected e.g TV, Magazines etc.
- Media Vehicles: It means the specific vehicles within each media are mentioned e.g. Sony in TV, Business Today among Magazines.
- Programme Choice: It means specifying the programmes like KBC on star plus or Brand equity the weekly supplement of Economic Times.
- No of Insertions: It means deciding the no of advertisements of the same size appearing in an individual medium per day, week, or month.
- Details: it contains major characteristics of the advertisement other than the copy and art work. It gives the size, specifications, the location specification etc.
- Timing: it details how the advertisement has to be scheduled over the campaign whether periodical, continuous, etc.

Principles of Media Scheduling

- Certain guidelines are necessary to make the media scheduling effective.
- **Perception:** what we see with our eyes is important but sometimes what we see through our selective perception is more important in deciding the issue.

Example full colour advertisement in newspaper compared with blank and white will be more effective.

- **Population**: The advertiser must have a fell for the audience and its needs, to decide on the correct media to put its advertisements across the people.
- **Media itself:** Identification of right media at right time is of utmost importance in making media scheduling effective.
- **Exposure:** The number of exposures will decide whether the audience persuasion has been achieved or not.

Methods of Media Scheduling: The various types of Media Scheduling are as under:

1. **Continuous schedule:** Here the advertising is evenly distributed over time. An advertisement runs steadily and on regular and continuous pattern without any gaps.

Example: Colgate toothpaste, surf excel, Amul etc.

Merits

a. It serves as constant reminder to the consumers.
b. It covers the entire campaign period without any seasonality.
c. It allows media priorities like quantity discounts, preferred location etc.

Demerits

a. This strategy is expensive.
b. Excessive exposure can bore the audience.
c. It results in limited media allocation.

2. **Flighting Schedule:** this method alternates the periods of advertising with periods of no advertising. Here advertiser spend heavy promotional expenditure during demand some other times there is no advertising expenditure

Example: advertisements on savings options to save tax appear more frequently near the close financial year and at the time of filing income tax returns.

Merits

a. It is cost efficient method.
b. It allows for inclusion of more than one medium of vehicle with limited budget.

Demerits

a. It results to low awareness and persuasion towards customers
b. Its results to competitive efforts during non scheduled periods
c. Increased likelihood of wear out.

3. **Pulsing schedule**: In this approach, the advertising is evenly distributed over time with frequent burst of heavy advertising. This method mixes continuous and flighting schedule approaches. Here advertiser heavy up advertisement during peak periods of selling.

Example: Automobile Industry, advertising is continuous throughout the year but may increase in September when new models are introduced.

Merits

a. It serves as constant reminder to consumers.
b. It covers the entire buying period.
c. It allows for media priorities.
d. Cost efficiency can be achieved.

Demerits

a. Limited media allocation is possible.
b. Lack of awareness, interest and retention of promotional messages.
c. Increased likelihood of wear out.

Other Scheduling Methods

a. **Bursting:** under this method, heavy advertising is done say 40-50% of the budget amount during a particular period say first second month and the remaining 60-50% of the advertisement budget may spent during remaining months of the year.

Example: Advertisement of Pumps during harvesting season of Paddy in summer.

b. **Road Blocking**: It means buying air time on all three networks simultaneously. Good many companies use this technique to give an impression to the viewers that the advertiser is all over the place.

b. **Blinking**: It is scheduling tactics which stretches its slim advertising budget over large audience through market segmentation. This is generally used in Restaurants and Inns for reaching sales People on Sunday & Saturday and for reaching business people on weekdays.

Difficulties in Media Selection

- Difficult in understanding Audience.
- Multiple option in Advertisement
- Proliferation of channel/Programme renders TV rating difficult.
- Low Involvement Viewers
- Overcrowding
- Intelligent media buying.

Media Vehicle Decision

- Deciding to include advertising in the communication mix process is a relatively easy decision compared to deciding which media and media vehicle (for example which magazine or which channel on TV, etc.).
- Most of the advertising budget gets spent on the media (and not the creative or production side). This is why a careful planning, negotiating and knowledge skills are very important. Expert media planners and buyers got the best out of the advertising by finding the right spaces or places for an ad campaign at the lowest cost.
- There are a wide variety of media available today for the advertisers to choose from. The decision is depended on a lot of factors at the same time it is a very crucial decision since the success of the campaign is highly depended on the media selection aspect.

Media vehicle choice is based on -

Quantitative Considerations of - Cost per Exposure

- **TV - unit of measurement**
- ***TRP*** x no. of exposures = ***GRP*** (gross rating points) / total no of exposures
- ***CPRP*** unit cost divided by TRP (cost per rating point)
- **Press - unit of measurement**
- ***Readership*** - total vehicle audience (higher than ***circulation)***
- ***CPT*** - unit cost divided by readership x 1000= CPT (cost per thousand)
- **Qualitative considerations of media vehicle choice**
- Editorial environment suitability.
- To gather media source effect copy approaches must vary by vehicle.

Types of Media Vehicles

1. **BROADCAST MEDIA:** Broadcast media are quite young in comparison to the printed word. Fundamentally there are two main forms of broadcast: television and radio.

Advertisers use these classes of media in order to reach mass audiences with their messages at a relatively low cost per target reached.

Advertising messages through the broadcast media use a small time period, normally 15 or 30 or 60 seconds depending on their budget and the availability.

2. **NARROWCASTING:** The word "narrowcasting" is particularly unique to the industry of media specifically that of broadcast media. It is, according to the dictionary, the ability to "aim a radio or TV program or programming at a specific, limited audience or consumer market. "For example, music television is presented on MTV (Music Television), or Channel V, CMM.ETC, CNN (Cable News Network) offers 24-hour news coverage; ESPN (Entertainment Sports Network) boasts an all sports format; and Star TV, Zee etc, covers the family entertainment segment.
3. **NEW MEDIA:** Recent technological advances have increased the range of new media available to the advertisers to communicate with their prospects and the consumers. New media allows for far greater level of interactions between the advertiser and the receiver.

The new media would include internet and short message service (SMS).

4. **INTERNET ADVERTISING:** The World Wide Web is a hybrid medium, which shares characteristics with mass communication as well as interpersonal communication. The medium combines the ability of the mass media to disperse a message to a wider audience with some of interpersonal communication's possibilities of feed-back and interaction.

Media Option Decisions

Media planner decides the ***unit of advertising***.

Starch scores throw light on unit impact.

- **Advertising size** – more impact rather than proportionate increase in readership
- **Colour** – adds 50% more readership.
- **Advertising location** – the end or beginning of string of commercial do better on recall.

Back / inside covers do better than inside mag. Pages.

- **Copy execution** – Ads that resemble editorial are read more.

Media Buying

1. Buying media units - space / time can be through
   - The AOR (agency of record)

- The creative agency
- In-house

2. Rates are negotiable depending on the supply and demand
    - Upfront buys
    - Scatter buys
3. Rates vary with specificity of the spot / position
    - RODP run of day part - TV
    - ROT run of time - radio
    - ROP run of paper – press – dailies

Model Questions

a. What is advertising? Why companies do Advertising?
b. Define Media.
c. Explain the Organization of Media Function.
d. Explain the role of media in Advertisement.
e. What is Media Budget? How Media Budget is set?
f. Explain the various factors to be considered for Media Budget.
g. Explain the various methods of Advertising/Media Budget.
h. What is Media Research? Explain the role of Media Research.
i. Explain the various types of media with their advantages and disadvantages.
j. What is Media Planning.
k. Explain the various factors influcing Media selection.
l. What is Media/Advertisement scheduling.
m. Explain the factors specifying media scheduling.
n. Explain the various methods of media scheduling.
o. Explain the difficulties in media selection.
p. Explain media vehicle decision.
q. What are various types of media vehicles?
r. What is Media Buying?